ESCAPE TO FREEDOM!

Night after night, Robert and Hannah discussed and discarded plans. Maybe they could travel by land and river to Beaufort, using their savings to bribe ferrymen and patrollers until they reached the Union lines. Maybe the *Planter*'s slave crew could overpower the three white officers and sail the boat to the Union fleet.

When they finally arrived at a solution it was so simple that Robert wondered why he hadn't thought of it before.

"One night when the officers are on shore, we're going to take the boat, put you and the children aboard and sail it out to the bar. With my wearing Captain Relyea's hat, the sentries'll think it's him and let us pass."

It was daringly simple, dangerously simple.

"And what'll happen if you're caught?" Hannah asked.

"I'll be shot," Robert spoke soberly. "Sure it's a risk. But freedom's only seven miles away. Freedom for Elizabeth, for Robert."

Hannah was silent, thoughtful. Then, "I'll go," she decided. "Where you die, I'll die."

CAPTAIN
of the
PLANTER:

The Story of
Robert Smalls

by DOROTHY STERLING

Illustrated by Ernest Crichlow

AN ARCHWAY PAPERBACK
POCKET BOOKS • NEW YORK

POCKET BOOKS, a Simon & Schuster division of
GULF & WESTERN CORPORATION
1230 Avenue of the Americas, New York, N.Y. 10020

Published by arrangement with Doubleday & Company, Inc.
Library of Congress Catalog Card Number: 58-5582

ISBN: 0-671-29851-8

First Pocket Books printing May, 1972

4th printing

Trademarks registered in the United States and other countries.

Printed in the U.S.A.

This book is for Linda and Michael Grigsby,
great-grandchildren of Robert Smalls

Contents

CAPTAIN
OF THE
PLANTER:
THE STORY OF
ROBERT SMALLS

———◆———

1.   The Day of the Hanging

The houses were empty, the kitchen fires unattended. There was no one in the stable, in the yard, on the street. Masters and coachmen, mistresses and cooks, houseboys, yard boys, house maids, ladies' maids—all were down on Craven Street to see the hanging. For two days carpenters had been building a scaffolding in the courtyard of the jail. For two days everyone had listened to the tap-tap of their hammers and had talked of nothing else.

Everyone was down on Craven Street to see the hanging—except Lydia Smalls. She was lying on her pallet in the deserted slave quarters, admiring her new-born baby. When the town bell rang, the infant stirred and began to cry.

"Hush, little baby," Lydia whispered. "The bell's singing, 'Howdy, Robert. Happy Birthday. Glad to greet you on this fine sunny day.' "

The baby balled his fingers into tiny brown fists and

1

waved them in the air. He arched his back and howled.

"Going to be a fighter," Lydia chuckled. "When you grow up you can say, 'I was born on the day of the hanging.' Even when everyone's forgotten the thief who was hanged they'll remember your birthday."

At last the little fists stopped waving. A mocking bird sang in the pecan tree in the yard. Sunlight and the sweet smell of jessamine drifted into the room and mother and son fell asleep.

The day of the hanging was April 5, 1839. The place was Beaufort on Port Royal Island, in St. Helena Parish, in the State of South Carolina, U.S.A.

Robert Smalls' birthplace was a small town with a big history. First it was the Spanish, following Columbus, who sailed along the southern shores of the new-found continent. They sent home reports of a maze of islands and bays and tidal rivers, of coastal plains rich in oak and pine and cedar, with stiff-leaved palmetto trees growing at the water's edge. There were deer and wild turkey and partridge in the forest, oysters and crabs, shrimp and giant terrapin in the coves and creeks.

One hundred years before the *Mayflower* reached New England the Spaniards dropped anchor in the finest harbor on the coast, Santa Elena, they called it. They carved crosses on the islands' oak trees and kidnapped the Indians to sell as slaves. Five years later they were back, with a boatload of Negro slaves, to build the first European settlement north of Mexico. But the slaves rebelled and ran off to the Indians, the sailors mutinied and the leader of the expedition died of fever.

2

On the heels of the Spaniards came the French, re-naming the spacious harbor Port Royal. The French blockhouse of logs and clay was destroyed by the Spanish. The Spanish fort that replaced it was burned by the Indians. It wasn't long before the three-cornered fight became four-cornered and the British took possession of the harbor.

By the beginning of the 18th century the province of Carolina was a prosperous string of settlements along the Atlantic coast. Charleston was the principal city while Beaufort, named after Henry, Duke of Beaufort, one of the British Lords Proprietors, was headquarters for the British fleet. The colonists exported rice and indigo, tar and turpentine, deer skins—and Indian slaves. They imported flour and beer, sugar and molasses—and Negro slaves.

British rule did not bring peace to the coastal plains and the islands along the sea. There were enemies everywhere, French, Spanish, Indian. There were enemies on the borders, and there were enemies within— the Negro slaves. By 1737 the Lieutenant Governor of the province was writing to London, "As our Negroes are very numerous and more dreadful to our safety than any Spanish invaders, there is an act of Assembly now preparing to have strong patrols established in all convenient districts. I am also sending for some Cherokee Indians to come down to the settlements to be an awe to the Negroes."

Every year there were rumors of slave rebellions. Every year there were reports of slaves shooting their masters, burning plantation houses or engaging in "the hellish practise of poisoning." Every year the planters' patrols were strengthened and the slave codes made more harsh. Disobedient slaves had their ears cut off, their noses split, their foreheads branded. Rebellious slaves were crucified or burned alive.

But still the colonists continued to import more slaves to work in their rice and indigo fields. By the time of the American Revolution there were three times as many Negroes as whites in South Carolina's low country. In 1775 there was a panic in Charleston when slaves echoed their masters' cries of "Liberty! Liberty!" Quickly the patriots imprisoned the shouting men. After the British occupied the coast, slaves flocked to their lines by the thousands—only to be herded onto sailing vessels and sold into slavery in the West Indies.

In the new United States there was talk of abolishing slavery. Were not all men created equal, with a right to life and liberty? Henry Laurens of South Carolina, president of the Second Continental Congress, said, "The time was when we solemnly engaged against further importation of slaves under a pretense of working by gradual steps a total abolition. We were then indeed in a religious mood and had appealed to God."

But a shrubby plant whose seeds are covered with fluffy white fibres proved to be more important than either the rights of man or the love of God. Before the Revolution there was scarcely any cotton grown in the American colonies. The seeds had to be picked out of the fibres by hand and a slave, working from dawn to dusk, could seldom clean more than a pound. Using the first crude cotton gin, he could clean fifty pounds. When the gin was harnessed to steam he could clean a thousand pounds of cotton in a single day.

It wasn't long before forests were chopped down, fields were cleared and the white flowers and bursting bolls of cotton blanketed the Southern countryside. On

5

the islands between Charleston and Savannah planters experimented with a new kind of cotton that had long, silky, cream-colored fibres. Sea Island cotton, used for the finest fabrics and strongest threads soon sold for two dollars a pound and the islands on which it was grown became the wealthiest farming region in the world.

A regiment of black-skinned workers armed with hoes or baskets, planted, thinned, weeded, and picked the golden crops. The bales of cotton piled higher on the city wharves and the slave regiments doubled, tripled, quadrupled. Charleston became a leading port and the country's principal slave market.

Scarcely anyone in South Carolina spoke of abolition any more. If he did, he was likely to be mobbed or thrown into jail. The rights of man were buried under eighty million pounds of cotton and God, the planters said, was on their side.

Our lives were one long eternal night, not even an occasional silver lining to bid us hope for a happier day.

Robert Smalls

2. Lydia Smalls

Lydia Smalls had never heard of Columbus or the Duke of Beaufort or the kings of France. But she knew cotton and she knew slavery. She was born in 1790 on Ashdale Plantation on Lady's Island, a half hour's row across the river from Beaufort and five hours' sail from Hilton Head at the entrance of Port Royal Bay. A long wooden bridge connected Lady's with St. Helena Island. A narrow creek separated it from Coosaw Island and the waterways leading to the Atlantic. It was a place of sand and marsh, of live oak trees bearded with Spanish moss, and flat broad fields where cotton grew.

As a baby, Lydia crawled on the dirt floor of a windowless, doorless cabin. Meals were eaten "on the hoe" in the fields, or out of a common pot in the firelit cabin after dark. There were no plates or spoons, no knives or forks. Nimble fingers plucked the strips of salt pork from the fire. An oyster shell served as scoop for the hot hominy, a gourd as dipper for the cool well water.

Before the morning star faded from the sky, the slave driver's horn called all hands to the fields. As a child, Lydia was a quarter-hand, working outdoors until the sun sank into the waters the Beaufort River and it was too dark to tell the weeds from the plants. On Saturdays she lined up in front of the overseer's house for her ration of corn and salt pork. On Sundays she ground the corn, washed her clothes and rested. Only at Christmas was there a cake of soap, a new blanket and a change of clothing.

Each Sunday all along the Street, as the row of slave cabins was called, young and old gathered around the bonfires to sing and talk. Sitting cross-legged with her eyes on the dancing flames, Lydia listened. This was her school.

There were men and women in the quarters who could still remember Africa and who spoke in the strange-sounding language of their native land. They told of their villages in the forest and of the passage across the big ocean in the slavers' crowded ships. Some of the younger hands, newly purchased in the Charleston slave mart, had come from Virginia and Maryland. To the African tales they added stories of big cities and fine houses, broad roads and fast ships, of the enormous country of which Lady's Island was a part.

Lydia drank it all in, forcing her eyes to stay open even when her head was nodding against her mother's shoulder. The world the young people described—the white men's world—was as foreign to her as the Africa of the old folks. Beaufort and Charleston seemed as far

8

away as the coast of Guinea, where her great-grand-mother had been born.

For Lady's Island, farmed by the Indians, named by the Spanish, explored by the French, settled by the English, was now a black island. The only white people living there were the overseers who managed the plantations. The low-lying fields and marshes and the cool breeze that blew in from the ocean were unhealthy, people said. The island was all right for slaves, but if white men—and their wives and children—moved there, they would surely take the fever and die.

Lydia had never spoken to a white woman or seen a white child. John McKee, the man who owned her from the tip of her bare toes to the top of her shiny black head, had his home in Beaufort. He rode to the plantation once a week or so, bringing rations, checking on the sick, striding through the fields to see how his cotton and his people were behaving. A few hours, and then he'd be gone. Only when the cotton was brought in from the fields to the gin house did he stay for so long as a day.

Mrs. McKee came at Christmas time, riding from the ferry landing in a fine carriage, followed by a wagon heaped high with clothes and blankets. If the crop had been good she brought oranges too, one for each slave child.

The children were shy when Mistress arrived. When she stepped down from her carriage, they ran and hid. Peeping through cracks in the cabin walls, they watched her slow progress along the Street. Even when they were called to come for the oranges, they buried their faces in their mothers' ragged dresses and scarcely dared look up. Not until her carriage was safely down the road again did they let loose their giggles and gossip about her shiny clothes and fur-trimmed bonnet and pale, pale skin.

Lydia had been timid when she was little, but she was bold now. She stared openly at the carriage, admired Mistress' dress and even remembered to say "Thank'ee" when an orange was placed in her hands.

"What's your name?" Mrs. McKee smiled down at her.

"Lydia."

"How old are you?"

For a moment Lydia was stumped. Most slave children didn't know their ages. They were born "at cotton-picking time" or "the year of the big storm." Nobody bothered to keep track of their birthdays. Then she remembered something she had heard around the fire.

"I was born the year after George Washington got President."

Mrs. McKee lifted her eyebrows and whispered to her husband. Lydia began to worry. Had she said something wrong? No, because Master patted her head and told her she was a good girl and Mistress gave her a second orange.

That was only the beginning. Next Sunday when Master brought the rations he asked for "the little girl who knows about George Washington." Helpful hands pushed her to the head of the line.

"Lydia"—his voice was kind—"I'm taking you back to live in Beaufort. Get your things together and be ready to leave when I'm finished here."

To live in Beaufort! It happened so quickly that Lydia didn't know whether to be glad or sad. A lump filled her throat as she kissed her mother good-bye, but when Master slung her astride his saddle she clutched the kerchief in which she'd wrapped her Sunday dress and Christmas soap and sat up straight. By the time they reached the ferry landing she was humming a song.

At first Beaufort seemed like heaven to the slave child. There were streets, not rutted and puddled like the island paths but covered with crushed oyster shells, gleaming white in the sunshine. There were neat gardens with shiny leaves in winter and sweet-smelling bright blossoms in spring. And the houses! For weeks Lydia walked on tiptoe when she entered Master's house.

There was so much to tell her mother when she visited the plantation on Sundays that Lydia couldn't remember it all. The food: chicken and stuffed turkey and roast goose, jellies and custards, iced cakes and candied orange peel. Whatever the McKees left on their platters was hers to feast on, and Maria, the cook, often warned of stomach aches-to-come.

There were the McKees' blue and white dishes, the silver trays, the knives and forks she quickly learned to use. The china basins and the pitcher from which she poured warmed water for the children's baths. The clock on the mantelpiece in the sitting room and the pictures of faraway places that hung on the parlor wall. And most remarkable of all, a mirror in a gilt frame that showed a picture of herself.

Of course, Lydia lived only in the shadow of this magnificence. In the yard behind the house, next to the outdoor kitchen and the stable, were the slave quarters. Lydia slept on the floor, alongside Maria and her husband, George, who was Master's coachman.

11

And of course, Lydia hadn't been brought to Beaufort just to see the sights. There were children to take care of: Caroline, Henrietta, Edward, Marguerite, and finally Henry, who was born when she was twenty-one. Endless tubs of water had to be heated, endless pinafores scrubbed. Small fingerprints must be wiped from the white wainscoting in the sitting room and washed off the windows in the parlor.

Mornings, there were steps to be swept and banisters dusted. Afternoons, she helped Maria in the kitchen. At dusk she set out the dishes on the sideboard and placed the damask napkins on the table before going upstairs to put the children to bed. By candlelight she scrubbed pots and polished silver in the outdoor kitchen.

Some Sundays she was too tired to make the trip to Lady's Island, and after her mother died she rarely visited the plantation. Instead, she went to church now, sitting in the slaves' gallery in a dress fashioned after Mistress' own.

As she grew from a bright-eyed, quick-tongued child to a slender woman there came a time when clothes and food and houses—white folks' clothes and food and houses—weren't enough. All kinds of feelings tumbled around inside of her. The beauty of Beaufort couldn't hide the ugliness of slavery. She hated to be sent on an errand to Craven Street for there, across from the Arsenal, was the slave mart. As she stood on the walk she could see human beings, men and women and children she knew, being auctioned off, sold to the highest bidder like so many sheep.

Next to the slave market was the jail. In its basement rooms slaves awaiting sale were chained to iron rings in the floor. In the jail yard Beaufort slaves were sent

to be whipped. Masters who were too soft-hearted to do the job themselves paid the jailer a few pence for each stroke of the lash. The slaves' screams could be heard even in the McKee yard. Some nights Lydia heard them in her dreams.

The older she grew the more she minded the constant cries of "Lyddie" from the McKee children. It was "Lyddie, do this," "Lyddie, fetch that." One day she turned on little Henry in a rage.

"My name is Lydia—Ly-di-a—and when you want me to do something say 'please.' "

"Lyddie, Lyddie, Lyddie," the little boy teased. "I can say anything I want. You're my slave."

"Henry, Henry, Henry," she retorted, and she slapped the child's face.

Even through his tears he remembered his power. "You call me 'Master Henry,' " he commanded, "or I'll tell my father and he'll have you whipped."

Lydia called him "Master Henry" and humbly begged his pardon. What could she do? She was grateful for the child's promise of silence and furious at her helplessness.

Sometimes she thought of running away. At dinner the McKees and their guests talked of the "damnable abolitionists" who helped slaves escape from their masters. But Beaufort was so very far from the North. How could she escape? She was too little, and the distance to freedom was too big.

For a few months one spring her hopes ran high. The quarters were buzzing with news from Charleston. On the second Sunday in July all the Negroes on the islands and in the city were to arm themselves and fight for their freedom. Before the day came, however, their plans were discovered and thirty-five of the leaders

14

were hanged in Charleston's jail yard. In Beaufort the town council met in secret session and doubled the number of armed men who patrolled the streets at night.

The years passed, and if Lydia frowned more than she laughed no one took notice. She was a good and faithful servant, and John McKee never regretted taking her from the cotton fields. When he died she became Master Henry's property, moving with him to the new house on Prince Street that he built for his bride.

It was in the slave quarters of Master Henry's new house that Lydia was lying on the day of the hanging. There was no one to bring gifts to her new brown-skinned baby, no one to care about him—except Lydia, and she cared fiercely. This child of her middle years must learn all the things she had wanted to learn, must travel to all the places she had wanted to go. Above all, he must have the one thing she prized most—freedom.

I never knew a man who wished himself to be a slave.
Abraham Lincoln

3. "... When I'm a Man"

A week after Robert's birth, Lydia was back at work,
stealing time between each task to run to her room and
make sure that her baby was all right. Soon he was a
toddler, scampering about the yard on sturdy brown
legs and shrieking with glee as he tried to pull the tail
feathers from the chickens or chased the turkeys that
roosted under the quarters.

For a few years Robert grew up like any Beaufort
boy. He climbed the pecan tree that shaded the outdoor
kitchen and fought the squirrels for the nuts. He hunted
the lizards that skittered across the glossy leaves of
the magnolias. He shinnied up the broad trunks of the
live oaks, making wigs and beards from the Spanish
moss that dripped from their branches.

He caught shrimps in the river at low tide, netted
crabs from the sea wall along Bay Street. He learned to
swim like the fish in the harbor and row like the fishermen. He spent long hours with the horses, riding them
bareback around the yard, racing with Eliza Jane,
Henry McKee's daughter.

16

A favorite spot after supper was the Arsenal, where the Beaufort Artillery drilled. They marched, shouldered arms, wheeled left and right with snap and precision while an audience of small boys looked on. Robert was delighted by the bright uniforms with their sparkling buttons and the music of the fife and drum.

Life was not all play. There were errands to be run for Mistress, boots to be blacked for Master. Robert helped George to groom the horses and he polished the door handles of the carriage until they shone.

Before breakfast he fetched water from the wooden pump down the street, trying to balance the bucket on his head the way the slave women did. Once he managed to walk all the way to the yard no-hands before the bucket tipped and the water spilled over his shirt. Lydia scolded, but Master, who was watching from the window, only laughed.

Each afternoon Robert carried in logs for the fireplaces and baskets of "fat wood," resinous pine knots that were used as kindling. He loved bringing wood to the Big House. First he walked along the path of bricks set into the ground. Then up the steps leading to the broad piazza, wiping his bare feet carefully before he crossed the waxed pine floors.

Each room had white-paneled walls, windows of real glass and ceilings so high that even a giant couldn't bump his head on them. From the ceilings hung chandeliers with hundreds of pieces of crystal that glittered when the wax candles were lit at night.

Parlor, sitting room, dining room, and that wasn't all. Carpeted steps and curving mahogany banisters led to a second floor where there were bedrooms with windows that looked out over the town. Robert stacked the logs neatly on the hearths in front of the big stone

17

fireplaces and sometimes found time for a game with Eliza Jane before Lydia called to him.

Even when he was out of sight, he was never long out of his mother's mind. She taught him manners, neatness, obedience, rapping his knuckles when he reached across the table for more meat without asking, cuffing him when he stained his Sunday shirt with the juicy blackberries that grew wild down the road, sending him supperless to the quarters when he went swimming before doing his chores. He learned to say "Yes, ma'am," "No, sir," and "Thank you" with a ready smile.

"Hold your head high," she'd tell him, "but don't be tonguey."

As he grew older, Robert was Master's slave as well as Lydia's boy. It was Robert who jumped from the high seat next to the coachman to open the carriage door for Master. It was Robert who helped carry the sacks of corn and sides of salt pork that Master brought to the plantation on Saturdays. And because Henry McKee liked the cheerful, talkative boy, it was Robert who carried his gun when he went hunting and who rowed the boat and baited the hooks when he fished. In the spring, when the drumfish were running in Beaufort River, Master and small slave spent long companionable hours together on the water. It took two pairs of hands to haul a four-foot fish over the side of the boat and two voices to exclaim over its size and fighting spirit.

It was after one of these day-long excursions that Robert, lying on the floor of their room, dreamed aloud to his mother.

"When I'm a man, I'm going to be just like Master. Going to have a house like his and a boat like his and

a plantation like his. Maybe I'll even marry Eliza Jane
and——"

Lydia sat bolt upright. "And have slaves like his?"
She began to shake the startled boy.

"No-o-o-m." Robert had never seen his mother so
upset.

" 'When I'm a man,' " she mimicked him. "You ain't
never going to be a man. You're a boy now and it'll
be 'boy,' 'boy,' 'boy' till you're sixty. When you're
stooped and limping along with a cane, you'll grow up
to be 'uncle.' 'Uncle Bob' they'll call you, same as
Eliza Jane calls me 'aunty.'

"You're never going to be a man because a man is
free. Free. And you're a slave. Think you're different than the plantation hands because Master lets you
row his boat? You haven't the sense of the slowest
quarter-hand on Lady's Island. You're black, same
as they. You're a slave, same as they. Only you——"

Words failed her and she cried. And with the tears
still wet on her cheeks she slapped Robert, "so's you'll
always remember what I'm saying." After a while
the sobbing boy fell asleep, but Lydia remained awake
through the night, tossing, turning, thinking.

She had failed. She had taught her boy to live in
the white man's world, but she had not taught him the
meaning of slavery. Until he understood this, he would
never—could never—win his freedom. By the time
the first faint rays of sunshine traveled through the
shuttered window, she had a plan.

When the two of them were finished with morning
chores, Lydia took Robert for a walk. As they passed
the Arsenal he began to tug at her arm, begging to
look through the arched doorway at the cannons in
the court.

19

"Arsenal's for white men." Her voice was harsh. "Don't s'pose they'd let a slave have a gun, do you?"

Her hand tightened around his when they reached the crowd in front of the slave mart. Robert had passed these auctions before. They were a part of everyday life in Beaufort. But the trembling, frightened people who stood on the block had nothing to do with him.

The auctioneer was pointing to a boy no bigger than Robert. "Could be you," Lydia whispered. "If Master died tomorrow you could be standing right there with your shirt off and those men poking and prodding you as if you were a horse. Maybe they'd sell you to Mississippi while I got shipped off to Texas."

Robert started to question, to argue, but this new idea was too overwhelming. As he watched, the boy on the block was sold to Mr. Fripp, Master's sister's husband. Robert resolved to visit him. He would ask him where he came from, where his mother was.

Lydia led him past the mart to the jail, boosting him to her shoulders so that he could look over the wall.

"Tell me what you see," she commanded.

He might have answered that he saw a tree that was unknown in North America until the white men landed there—a whipping tree. A woman's wrists were tied to its lowest branches. A lash whistled through the air and landed on her bare back, her shoulders, her arms. Once, twice, more times than Robert could count. He begged his mother to put him down.

"No." Her voice sounded strange. "Wait till it's done."

The boy tried to turn his head away, to blot out the sight, but no matter how tightly he screwed up his eyes, he could still hear the woman's screams. At last it was over. The jailer untied her wrists and she fell to the ground. As he carried her away, Robert caught a glimpse of her face. It was Susannah, whom he met at the pump each morning when he went to fetch water.

He was sobbing so when Lydia put him down that they walked all the way home before she could quiet him. Even her comfort was cold, because she *had* to tell him, "It could happen to me. It could happen to you. Master and Mistress are good, but slavery— slavery is bad."

Late in the afternoon Robert slipped away to visit the Fripps. In the quarters he found Frederick, the boy he'd seen on the auction block. In March, Frederick had been in Maryland with his mother and father, his sisters and brothers. Then, with iron circlets around his ankles, he had traveled in the hold of a ship from Baltimore to Charleston and from Charleston to Beaufort. Now it was April and he would soon be on St. Helena Island working in the cotton fields. It was so quick and confusing that he sat dazed, barely able to answer questions.

Robert's education was well under way. One Saturday when he traveled with Master to Lady's Island he asked permission to stay overnight at Ashdale and return home alone the next day. Other weeks when he stood in front of the overseer's house, next to Henry McKee, he had hardly noticed the field hands. He'd been busy measuring out corn, counting the rations of salt pork. He and Master. The hands even nodded their heads and thanked *him* when he scooped corn into their baskets.

Today it was as if he were seeing them for the first time. They stood patiently in line, their faces blank and expressionless. No one jostled or pushed. A few

21

talked with Master when their turn came. Others only grunted and turned away. If Robert had known the words he might have called them stolid or even sullen.

Then, when Master had ridden down the road, everything was different. The blank faces came alive, talked, laughed, argued, and grumbled. "Mighty small piece o' pork he's giving out this week," one young man said.

"Ssh!" A woman nudged him and jerked her head toward Robert.

Robert could feel his cheeks burning. Outside the gin house boys and girls were whispering and giggling. He was sure they were laughing at him.

A pig-tailed girl left the group and planted herself in front of him. "They say you're Master's boy. Are you?"

Robert's eyes fell under her bold stare. "I-I-guess so," he stammered. "At least——"

An older woman came to his rescue. "Ain't you Lydia Smalls' son?"

The boy nodded.

"Would of knowed you anywhere. Same eyes, same perky way o' holding your head. Your ma and I were girls together right here at Ashdale. Likely you heard her talk o' Chloe Barnwell."

Robert found his tongue. His mother had told him to be sure to ask for Chloe Barnwell. Under her sponsorship he was soon accepted by the boys and girls. He ate supper with Bess, the pig-tailed girl who had questioned him, and he slept in Chloe's cabin, along with her grown children and three small grandchildren.

The boys and girls weren't very different from Beaufort children. They liked to climb trees and go fishing just as he did. But the way they lived! When he thanked Bess's mother after supper, he was glad that she couldn't know how hungry he still felt. Bess and her brother had never tasted turkey or beef, any baked goods except hoe cakes, any sweetening except molasses. When he told them about the frosted layer cakes Maria baked they thought he was fooling—or boasting.

Lying awake on the dirt floor in Chloe's cabin after everyone else was asleep, Robert thought of the room he shared with his mother. It wasn't grand compared with the McKee house, but it had whitewashed walls and a rough wood floor and shutters to cover the window openings when it rained. And there were only two people in it instead of nine!

Any feelings of superiority he might have had disappeared the next day when he joined the bonfires along the Street. At first he had trouble understanding the plantation hands' speech. They spoke faster than the people in Beaufort did, using unfamiliar words like "buckrah" for "white man" and "dayclean" for "daybreak" and saying "enty?" at the end of a sentence when they meant "isn't that so?" But he soon got the hang of it, finding what they said more important than how they said it.

Will, one of the oldest hands on the plantation, had learned to read when he was a boy. Every scrap of printed matter, even if it was only the labels from the patent medicines Master brought for the sick, were saved for him to translate. Gabriel and Phyllis, recent arrivals from Charleston, could also read. Between the three of them they explained the news of the day. "Politicking," they called it.

For the first time the boy heard of Frederick Douglass, who had escaped from slavery a few months before Robert's birth. Now Douglass was editing his own newspaper and making speeches against slavery in New York and Boston and even in London, far across the sea. Gabriel, who had a copy of one of Douglass' latest talks, read from it haltingly:

" 'The law gives the master absolute power over the slave. He may work him, flog him, hire him out, sell him, kill him. In law, the slave has no wife, no children, no country and no home. He can own nothing, possess nothing, acquire nothing, but what must belong to another.

" 'He toils, that another may reap the fruit; he is industrious, that another may live in idleness; he eats unbolted meal, that another may eat the bread of fine flour; he labors in chains at home, under a burning sun and a biting lash, that another may ride in ease and splendor abroad.

" 'He lives in ignorance, that another may be educated; he rests his toil-worn limbs on the cold, damp ground, that another may repose on the softest pillow; he is clad in coarse and tattered raiment, that another may be arrayed in purple and fine linen; he is sheltered only by the wretched hovel, that a master may dwell in a magnificent mansion.' "

A slave wrote this! The words spun round in Robert's mind as he walked the three miles to the ferry landing where a bateau would carry him across the river to Beaufort. Back home he could think of nothing else. It was late in the evening when he told Lydia about his visit.

"Ma, ma. . . ." He hesitated, embarrassed. "When I grow up I'm going to be like Frederick Douglass. I'm going to be a man."

In the dark, Lydia stroked her boy's hair and

smiled. At last he was on the road that would lead to freedom.

Almost every week now, Robert stayed over at Ashdale. When he came home even Master noticed the change in him.

"Boy's getting bad-tempered," he complained to Lydia. "Grumbles and mutters under his breath when I ask him to fetch something. Afraid he's spoiled."

Mistress thought that it was spring fever and ordered a daily dose of sulphur and molasses. The matter might have rested there if it had not been for the bronze bell that hung in the jail.

Every day at sunset the bell rang to warn the slaves that it was time to get off the streets until morning. Although Robert had obeyed the curfew bell all his life it suddenly seemed to have a special message for him.

"Get along home, Robert," it tolled. "Go home, slave boy. At night the streets are for free men."

One summer evening Robert made up his mind to dare the bell. Without a thought for the consequences, he slipped out of the yard while his mother was busy in the kitchen. He walked all the way to Bay Street before the patrollers caught him. They threw him into jail, where Master had to call for him the next morning and pay a fine for his release. More puzzled than angry, McKee tried to find out why the boy had behaved this way. But Robert only shrugged his shoulders. How could he explain to Master?

Lydia needed no explanations. The curfew bell had tolled its message for her too. She was troubled, however, about her boy's future. Only the other day she had heard Master talking to Mr. De Treville. There had been a disastrous drop in the price of cotton and Master had made unwise investments, besides. He was planning to sell the Prince Street house to De Treville and move to smaller quarters on Carteret Street. When this happened, what would he do with Robert?

She put the question to Master a few nights later. He was sitting on the piazza smoking his after-dinner cigar. Mistress, who hated the smell of cigar smoke, had already retired.

"Been wondering about the boy." McKee leaned back in his rocker. "George's getting on and I'd always thought someday Robert'd be coachman. Way things are going now, though, don't know as I can keep him on, just waiting for George to die."

"Then send him to Charleston." Lydia blurted out the words. "He's a good worker, none better for his age. He'll take a job and pay you his wages."

"Let him hire his time, eh?" McKee chewed the tip of his cigar thoughtfully. "He's smart, all right, and to tell the truth I could use the cash right now. But, Lyddie, the way he's been acting lately—a crazy thing like this curfew business—I'm afraid he'll get in trouble in Charleston. People there don't stand for nonsense."

"There'll be no nonsense," Lydia assured him. "I'll have a talk with him. He's a good boy, only a mite spoiled."

There was little more said about it, but in the fall when Mistress bustled about, preparing for Master's trip to Charleston, Lydia spent long evenings washing, sewing, ironing, so that her boy would have clean clothes for his new life.

Early one morning Master's shiny portmanteau and Robert's worn carpetbag were placed side by side on the roof of the carriage. Farewells were brief. If the boy didn't turn back to see the tears in his mother's eyes, well, she had looked ahead too when she'd ridden John McKee's horse to the Beaufort ferry on that day so long ago.

All along the broad Shell Road to the city, past the pink crepe myrtle bushes that fringed the streets and the scarlet-leaved gum trees in the swamps, past withering stalks of cotton and low-lying fields of rice, master and slave thought their separate thoughts. Master was rehearsing his talk with the cotton broker, hoping for a good price for this year's crop. Slave was remembering his mother's words:

"Work hard. Don't be tonguey. Grow to be a man."

Charleston was rich, powerful, aristocratic, arrogant, and dictatorial.

C. C. Coffin, *Freedom Triumphant*

4. Growing Up in Charleston

The horses' hoofs sounded like thunder to Robert when the carriage crossed the Ashley River bridge the following day. Turning his head from side to side, he tried to take in all the wonders of the city at once.

There were shops and banks and tall church spires, cobblestoned streets and brick-paved alleyways. And the people! Robert had never seen so many on the streets at one time. Aproned tradesmen bowing to crinolined ladies, . white-turbaned slave nurses with their charges, street vendors balancing baskets of vegetables on their heads or pushing wheelbarrows piled high with shrimp and she-crabs.

The boy's eyes were bright with excitement when George pulled the horses to a halt in front of a red-brick house below Broad Street. He caught a glimpse of tiled roofs and ironwork balconies, of windows shuttered against the midday sun. This was the home of Mistress' sister, Mrs. Eliza Ancrum, where Robert was to board during his Charleston stay.

There was scarcely time to stretch his cramped legs in the slave quarters behind the walled-in garden before Master called him. Together they walked up King Street to the office of the city contractor. Robert was hired to work as a lamplighter for four dollars a month.

"Four dollars," Master repeated as they left the office. "Mind you give it to Mrs. Ancrum on the first of each month."

Two weeks later, when Master had completed his business and departed for home, Robert already felt a part of the busy city. With a rag slung over his shoulder and a ladder hooked under his arm he traveled from street corner to street corner to wipe out the lamp globes and clean the soot from the jets. In the afternoons he made the same trip again, armed with a long taper with which to light the lamps. When the bells of St. Michael's Church rang out the curfew, he was still on the street with his taper and matches, putting stars of light atop each iron post. A copper identification tag around his neck and a pass in his pocket protected him from the patrollers if they stopped to question him.

Work took up only a part of his time. There were hours left for standing with nose pressed against the windows of shops, for running through the twisting alleyways and walking along the broad streets. On Sundays he traveled to the outskirts of the city, to the railroad station where steam locomotives puffed their way to the state capital at Columbia, or to the race track, where Carolina society gathered to place its bets and cheer its favorites.

Eager, inquisitive, the twelve-year-old boy asked questions of everyone he met—the vendors whose cries of "Raw Shrimp" and "Porgy" echoed through the downtown streets, the boys playing ball in the alleys, the servants with whom he shared a room at the Ancrums'. Was slavery different here than it was in Beaufort?

"Who you suppose made those fine iron gates next door?" old Scipio lectured him. "Slave iron mongers. Who you suppose baked the brick for the garden walls and laid it up so straight and true? Who built the houses and churches the chivalry are so proud of? Slave masons, carpenters, glaziers."

There was a slave harness-maker with his own shop on Meeting Street. There were slave blacksmiths and butchers, barbers and butlers, cooks and caterers, painters, plasterers, pilots. There were also free Negroes who had worked and saved to buy themselves. Henry Jones, a free Negro, operated a livery stable on King Street. Eliza Lee, a free Negro, owned the Mansion House, a fashionable inn on Broad Street.

Free Negroes paid taxes on property valued at many thousands of dollars, owned carriages, horses—and sometimes slaves. There were more than four thousand free Negroes in Charleston in 1851, yet even these free men were required to wear identifying tags around their necks as Robert did, and to have a white man act as their "guardian."

Was slavery different here than it was in Beaufort? Robert watched the sales of slaves on the street corners and in the alleys of downtown Charleston. He peered through the barred windows of Ryan's three-story slave jail on Queen Street.

"They's whipping posts in there and a treadmill that makes you walk round and round till you're so tired you fall out," a street vendor told him. "And the cells are dark as night."

A buzzard circled overhead, flying low as it neared the butchers' stalls on Market Street. For a moment the shadow of the bird's broad wings covered the vendor's face. Robert shivered.

Down the street from Ryan's jail, at the corner of Church and Queen, was the Planters Hotel. Three stories high, with brick pillars and delicate ironwork balconies, it was as elegant as the jail was dismal. Foreign visitors stayed there, and planters and their families who came to town for the gay social season.

Learning that the hotel had an opening as a waiter, Robert presented himself at the side door and asked for the job. He was hired so quickly that he had no time to worry about what Master would say. But Master laughed, as he usually did, and took the extra dollar that the boy now earned. Neither mentioned the coppers that were sometimes tossed at him. These were his, to jingle in his pocket and to spend on ground-nut cakes and stick candy.

Waiting on tables and carrying trays up the narrow stairs to the bedrooms was harder than the outdoor life of a lamplighter. Now a damask napkin was slung over Robert's arm and in his hands he carried a brimming soup tureen or a bottle of rich red claret. All day long and until late at night it was "Boy, fetch this," "Boy, tote that," and sometimes "Clumsy boy, can't you watch out!"

After the dishes had been cleared from the tables and the gentlemen were smoking their cigars and sipping their brandy, Robert stood in the shadow of the patio wall and listened to their talk. If he were ever to change from "boy!" to man, there was much he had to learn from white Charleston.

These men in the brightly lit dining room were the "chivalry," the aristocratic rulers not only of Charleston society, but of all South Carolina. And South Carolina was the state that owned the most slaves, fought the hardest for what they called "the peculiar institution," and wielded the most influence in the halls of Congress and the White House.

Not satisfied with their present slaveholdings, they hoped to see slavery in all the new territories, in the lands of the Louisiana Purchase, in Kansas and Nebraska and Texas. Listening to them thump the table and declare that cotton was king—that Northern factories would collapse without the South's fluffy white fibres—Robert was troubled. They were so confident, so sure of themselves and their cause.

More and more often in his free hours, he turned his footsteps to the waterfront. Charleston was a finger of land, bounded by the Cooper River on the north and the Ashley on the south, with the Atlantic Ocean lapping at the sea walls which lined its eastern shore. The blue waters of the harbor were dotted with islands and bristling with forts. James Island, Morris Island, Folly, where there were cotton plantations and the summer homes of rich planters. Fort Johnson and Fort Moultrie, whose guns chased away the British in 1776; Castle Pinckney, built when war with France was feared; and the half-finished Fort Sumter rising from a sand spit in the harbor's main channel.

From the Battery on a clear day, Robert could see brigs and schooners and square-rigged clipper ships anchored at the bar, seven miles out. They were waiting for high tide and a pilot boat to guide them through

the narrow channel of deep water to the city's docks. Along East Bay Street, where the wharves jutted out into the Cooper River, he watched the ships come in. Ships from Liverpool, Boston, New York, Norfolk, unloading casks and boxes, dumping their ballast of cobblestones, and then filling their holds with bales of cotton.

There was a hidden cargo, too, that passed from hand to hand and mouth to ear. The steward of the *James Adger,* five days out of New York, brought the latest issue of the *Liberator,* New England's abolitionist newspaper. The wheelsman of the *Kiawah* had a copy of *Uncle Tom's Cabin* in his sea bag. The cabin boy from *Pride of India,* whose last port of call had been the West Indies, told Robert stories of the free black republic of Haiti that made the thirteen-year-old's eyes grow round with pride and wonder.

After two years in Charleston, Robert grew restless. He had had enough of the chivalry at the Planters Hotel and he longed for the freer life of the waterfront. When he was in Beaufort at Christmas time he asked Master's permission to change jobs. For a year and a half he drove a hoisting-horse on the wharves, guiding the bales of cotton as they were lifted from the pier to the high decks of the steamers. By the time he was fifteen he had been made foreman, boss of a crew of blue-shirted stevedores.

Restless again, bored with the routine of the docks, he moved on to John Simmons' sailing loft to learn the trade of sailmaker and rigger. Most of the cotton that reached Charleston's warehouses was transported by water from the islands and coastal plantations and most of the cotton boats—sail and steam—were outfitted in Simmons' yard.

Robert sewed sails, painted hulls and cabins and
scraped barnacles and seaweed from fouled-up lines.
When there was rigging to be done, he shinnied up
the masts and, with his legs wrapped around the smooth
pine poles, attached the stays and secured the ropes.

After the sails were hoisted, the rigging had to be
tested in all sorts of wind and weather before the
boats were delivered to their owners. This was the
work Robert liked best. Watching the pilots, talking
with them when the day's work was done, he began to
handle the boats with skill and assurance.

"That boy's got the makings of a pilot," John Simmons boasted to one of his customers. "Ever see him
at the bar when the tide's going out? 'Stead of dropping
anchor and waiting for high water he just backs up
the ship and rides right in with the swell."

"That boy" was now seventeen years old, with other
problems on his mind besides cotton boats. He studied
his reflection in the window of a shop on Meeting
Street as he walked home. Five feet five. Not tall certainly, but broad-shouldered, slim-waisted, and with
an air of strength and self-confidence. With a damp-
ened finger, he smoothed the edges of a brand-new
moustache and the wispy chin hairs of what would
someday be a goatee. After supper, he must mend the
torn pocket on his pants and ask Charlotte, the Ancrums' house maid, to press them.

"What you need's a wife," Charlotte grumbled as
she slid the flat iron along his trousers.

Robert had been thinking the same thing. He needed
a wife to iron his shirts and pants, but her eyes must
sparkle when she laughed the way Hannah Jones' did.
Hannah, whose black curls brushed against his cheek
when they danced, merry Hannah, madcap Hannah,

who had a daring that matched his own, and a quiet wisdom that reminded him of his mother.

For six months they had spent their Sundays together, meeting at the Negro church, where they could sit in pews instead of in the slave gallery, walking in White Point Gardens at the Battery, riding the ferry to Sullivan's Island with a basket lunch. They made a handsome couple, and people paused to look at them.

"See those two." A white lady nudged her husband. "Not a care in the world."

"No worries like we have," he agreed. "Don't have to think where their next meal's coming from. It's the slaves own us, not we them."

At just that moment Robert was kicking a pebble along the beach and repeating, "How we going to live if we get married? There's you at the Kingmans'. There's me at the Ancrums'. We see each other Saturday nights, Sundays. Where do we go in the winter when it's too cold to walk in the park or sit on the beach? Why, even a bear——"

Hannah patted his hand. "I know," she finished for him. "Even a bear has a cave to live in and raise a family. You said that before, a hundred times," she teased.

"Only thing to do"—Robert came back to the subject over lunch—"is to save till I can buy your freedom. And then——"

"And then——" It was Hannah's turn to sound angry. "And then we'll be old and gray. No. If Master'll let me hire my time, somehow we'll make enough extra money to rent a room together."

The argument rumbled on all summer until Hannah's plan won out. If Henry McKee would accept a monthly payment of fifteen dollars from his slave, Robert, and if Samuel Kingman would accept a monthly payment of seven dollars from his slave, Hannah, then all the young couple had to do was to earn a sufficient sum above that for their living expenses. When both masters agreed to the arrangement and gave permission for the marriage, it boiled down to a problem in simple arithmetic—or higher mathematics.

With their wages promised to their masters how were they to live? The answer was to be found at the waterfront, where sailors who had been weeks at sea were glad to pay Hannah for laundering their clothes and to buy the chickens and strawberries and fresh eggs that Robert brought over from the islands. The answer was to be found at the Mills Hotel, where Hannah, now working as a chambermaid, could get food for their suppers and occasional gifts of clothing from the ladies she served. The answer was to be found in giving up Sunday picnics so that Robert could work as a deck hand on an excursion steamer and Hannah do extra sewing for her ladies. When they found two rooms above a livery stable on East Bay Street which they could have if Robert cleaned the horses' stalls, the arithmetic problem was solved.

On December 24, 1856, in the yard of Henry McKee's Carteret Street home in Beaufort, Hannah Jones and Robert Smalls were married. Gray-haired old George gave away the bride while Master supplied food and punch for everyone. In the evening the wedding guests set off the rockets and Roman candles with which South Carolina celebrated its snowless Christmas.

As the fireworks lit up Robert's face, Lydia looked at her son. It should have been the happiest moment of his life—but it wasn't. Despite happiness and hard work there was a feeling deep inside him that he couldn't hide. A feeling that welled up again when he returned to the familiar scenes of Beaufort. Perhaps the name for it was shame.

Hannah was his wife, but she was Samuel Kingman's slave. Hannah was his wife, but she belonged to Samuel Kingman. He was almost eighteen years old, sailmaker, rigger, pilot, husband. But he was not yet a man.

They say the Negro has no rights a white man is bound to respect, but it seems to me they send men to Congress and pay them eight dollars a day for nothing else but to talk about the Negro.

Harriet Tubman

5. The Darkening Sky

Painfully, the young couple gathered together the pieces that went into a home. A table and four rickety chairs. A few chipped dishes. An old brass bedstead, the first bed that either of them had ever slept in. Some mornings there was no food in the house for breakfast, some evenings the last stub of candle spluttered and died before Hannah had finished with the laundry.

But they were young and healthy and the happy days outnumbered the troubled ones. Once, when there were no more candles in the house a lady gave Hannah an old kerosene lamp with fuel enough to last the week. Often fishermen would give Robert a bucket of oysters or a fine string of porgies in return for work on their boats. Always, there were friends dropping by to admire the fine light that the lamp gave, to share the tasty oysters, or to bring a pot of stew and a basket of greens when the Smalls' cupboard was bare.

Their friends were house servants and skilled workers, free and slave, from all parts of Charleston. Sitting around the scarred wooden table as the evening drew late, one of them was sure to ask, "What's happening in the country? What news from Washington and Kansas?"

There was a storm approaching, and its fierce winds could be felt even in the little rooms on East Bay Street. At the heart of the storm was slavery. The North against the South, fighting on the plains of Kansas to decide whether the territory should be free or slave. The North against the South, debating in the halls of Congress. The North against the South, battling in the newspapers and at the polls. With each passing month, the clouds of war moved nearer.

Only last year Congressman Brooks of South Carolina had beaten Senator Sumner of Massachusetts over the head with a cane, leaving him bloody and insensible on the Senate floor. While Northerners sputtered with rage, South Carolina's chivalry gave Brooks a banquet and a new cane inscribed, "Hit him again."

Only last year the brand-new Republican Party had nominated John C. Frémont for President with the slogan, "Free Soil, Free Labor, Free Men, Frémont." Rumors spread through Charleston's kitchens and alleyways. If Frémont were elected the slaves would be freed. If Frémont were elected— But not one single vote was cast for him in all of South Carolina, and it was James Buchanan, the slaveholders' candidate, who became President instead.

Now all Charleston was buzzing over the Dred Scott case. Scott was a slave who sued for his freedom when his master took him to live in a free state. His case had dragged through the courts for ten years until it reached the Supreme Court in Washington. Chief Justice Taney, a Maryland slaveholder, denied Scott's appeal. Congress, he announced, had no power to declare any soil free, anywhere, at any time. Besides, "the unhappy black race" were "beings of an inferior order . . . articles of merchandise" with "no rights which the white man was bound to respect."

Again, while the South applauded, the North was outraged. In Illinois, a lanky lawyer left his desk to speak to the people of his state. Abraham Lincoln was no abolitionist, but he feared the spread of slavery to the territories. "A house divided against itself cannot stand," he said. "I believe this government cannot endure permanently half slave and half free. It will become all one thing, or all the other."

In New York State, Frederick Douglass advised his readers to meet the decision "in a cheerful spirit. This very attempt to blot out forever the hopes of an enslaved people may be one necessary link in the chain of events leading to the complete overthrow of the whole slave system."

In Charleston, it was not always easy to keep up a cheerful spirit. Chief Justice Taney's words burned themselves into Robert's mind. "No rights which the white man was bound to respect." A year later he flung them at Hannah, thumping his fist on the table until she begged him to be quiet.

"It's her I'm thinking about." He brought his voice down to a whisper. "She's——"

A cry from the old brass bed interrupted him. "She" was Elizabeth Lydia Smalls, born February 12, 1858. She was a pretty baby, but——

"An article of merchandise." Robert stared gloomily at her. "She's not our baby. She's Samuel Kingman's property. He can take her away any time he wants. Whip her. Sell her. Send her to Ryan's jail."

Hannah trembled, close to tears. There was no use repeating that Mr. Kingman had been a kind master as masters went, that he wouldn't do any of these things to their tiny girl. According to the laws of South Carolina and the decision of the Supreme Court of the United States, what Robert said was true.

All night long she listened to Robert's restless footsteps. At eight the next morning he was across the city, knocking at the Kingmans' door. When he returned there was a smile on his face and a piece of paper in his hand. Slowly, he spelled out the words:

"I hereby agree to sell my slave, Hannah Jones Smalls, and my slave, Elizabeth Lydia Smalls, to Robert Smalls for the sum of $800.

SAMUEL KINGMAN"

Eight hundred dollars! Hannah tried to hide her dismay. Little Elizabeth would be a grown woman before they could scrape together so huge a sum. But Robert didn't notice. He was determined to be the best pilot and the sharpest trader and the hardest worker in all of Charleston.

At night he pored over maps and charts, tracing the channels with a stubby forefinger, memorizing the location of shoals and reefs. By day he studied currents and tides. Twice each twenty-four hours the water raced out of the coastal creeks and rivers to the sea, leaving boats aground on the sandy bars. Twice each twenty-four hours it flowed back again, thudding against the bulkheads of the piers, floating the stranded boats. A seaman had to know the tides in each river and bay, to judge when to drop anchor and when to race the ebbing water back to shore.

Soon Robert was delivering boats to plantations on the islands along the coast, threading his way through the harbor channel to the open waters of the Atlantic or sailing through the Stono River and the narrow inland waterways all the way to Beaufort. In the summer, when Simmons' business slackened, Robert worked as a wheelsman on a coasting schooner.

There were times when he was too tired to sleep at night and too tired to get up in the morning, times when he felt as if he were on the treadmill in Ryan's jail. But in a year he and Hannah had saved two hundred dollars; in two years, four hundred dollars; and by the spring of 1861, they had more than seven hundred dollars hidden away under a loose board in the floor.

By the spring of 1861, however, the clouds of war were directly overhead. It was too late for a slave to dream of buying freedom—too late or too early.

All during the warm summer of 1861 men tramped the streets in Northern cities singing:

> *"Old Abe Lincoln came out of the wilderness,*
> *Out of the wilderness, out of the wilderness,*
> *Old Abe Lincoln came out of the wilderness,*
> *Down in Illinois."*

Northern newspapers wrote of "Honest Abe, the Rail Splitter," but in the South he was called "an ugly baboon," "an African gorilla," a "black Republican." With the help of his running mate, Hannibal Hamlin, who was "a free Negro," the Southern papers said, he would surely free the slaves.

There were men in South Carolina who hoped to see slavery grow more and more powerful. They dreamed of reopening the African slave trade, now forbidden by law, of building a confederacy of slaveholders that would reach to the Amazon River in South America. They were delighted with Lincoln's candidacy because it gave them just the excuse they needed for rebellion. On the day after Lincoln was elected President, these hotheads thronged the streets of Charleston, shaking hands and congratulating each other on the Republican victory.

Six weeks later they met in St. Andrew's Hall on Broad Street and unanimously voted that "The union now subsisting between South Carolina and other states under the name of the United States of America is hereby dissolved." In the evening they marched to meet the Governor at Institute Hall. One by one, they walked to the front of the room to sign the parchment sheet on which the articles of disunion were inscribed. Then the chairman's voice boomed out:

"I proclaim the State of South Carolina to be an independent commonwealth."

Two blocks away Robert and Hannah would hear the roar that went up from the crowded hall. While the bells of St. Michael's played "Auld Lang Syne," cannons boomed and barrels of tar were rolled out into the streets and set ablaze. All night long men visited the beer gardens to drink to the Independent State of South Carolina.

When Robert went to work in the mornings he saw red-sashed companies of volunteers drilling in the streets and banners declaring, "Resistance to Lincoln is Obedience to God."

South Carolina hastened to break all ties with the Union. Federal judges resigned from their judgeships. U. S. Congressmen left their seats in the House and Senate. Frontier guards were stationed at the state's borders and the newspapers labeled all news from the North as "Foreign News." Three days after the articles of secession were signed the Stars and Stripes was lowered from the flagstaff above the Customs House and South Carolina's palmetto flag raised in its stead.

The cannon on the Customs House lawn was shot off so frequently in those troubled months that Elizabeth learned to clap her hands and cry "Boom-boom" when she heard it. A six-gun salute when Mississippi seceded. Twelve guns for Florida and Alabama. Then Georgia, Louisiana, and the loudest burst of all when the Confederacy was formed and Jefferson Davis elected its President. At the State House in Montgomery, Alabama, when he took the oath of allegiance, an actress danced on the Union flag while the Confederates' Stars and Bars waved from the top of the flagpole.

By the time Lincoln moved into the White House in March, the Rebels had taken over federal property all over the South—coastal forts and navy yards, custom houses and post offices, lighthouses, hospitals, arsenals, and even the mint in New Orleans where U. S. money was coined. Charleston militia companies in new gray uniforms seized the federal arsenal with its stand of seventy thousand arms and marched into Fort Moultrie, Fort Johnson, and Castle Pinckney to the music of their regimental bands.

It looked like a bloodless victory. The Yankees

were too cowardly to fight, people said. Except, perhaps, at Fort Sumter in Charleston Harbor, where Major Robert Anderson of the U. S. Army was still in command of the Union garrison.

Fort Sumter, rising sixty feet above the waves in the center of a half-circle of Rebel forts, could not hope to hold out for long. Major Anderson had eighty-five officers and men, General Beauregard, Rebel commander in Charleston, more than five thousand troops. Major Anderson had provisions for only a few more days and he was no longer allowed to buy food in Charleston's market. Federal ships left New York with supplies for the besieged garrison, but before their arrival Beauregard presented Anderson with an ultimatum:

"I am ordered by the Government of the Confederate States to demand the evacuation of Fort Sumter."

Excitement mounted in Charleston. On the night of April 12, Robert tossed and turned, unable to sleep. He could hear ammunition wagons rumbling over the cobblestones and the tramp, tramp of marching feet. Midnight, two o'clock, four. He kept time by St. Michael's chimes. Suddenly, from the harbor, there was the booming of a cannon. A screaming shell rose from Fort Johnson, arching across the sky to bury itself in Sumter's thick brick walls.

With no thought for the patrollers, Robert hastily dressed and ran down to the Battery. The harbor was like a gigantic theater with all Charleston as audience. As exploding shells lit up the scene, carriages and horses jammed the streets. Women swarmed to the housetops, climbing atop chimneys for a better view, and small boys jumped from roof to roof for front-row seats.

When the wind rolled back the smoke, the spectators could see Union ships anchored off the bar. Hampered by rainy weather and outgunned by the ring of Rebel batteries, the Northern vessels were too late to help Major Anderson and his men.

All day, all night, and for thirty-four long hours, the bombardment continued until the mighty fortress was in ruins, its walls breached in a hundred places. Anderson's food and ammunition were used up, his barracks a heap of broken brick. There was nothing left to do but surrender.

On Sunday April 14, Robert and Hannah watched Major Anderson and his blue-coated soldiers march from the fort with their flag flying and their band playing "Yankee Doodle." As the steamer *Isabel* carried them to the Union vessels off the bar, Abraham Lincoln called for 75,000 volunteers to put down the rebellion. The war of words was over. The war with guns had begun.

The Master run, ha ha!
The slave he stay, ho ho!
It must be now the kingdom come
And the year of jubilo.

Civil War song

6. What's in Store for Us?

When the Stars and Bars which the ladies of Charleston had sewn for the occasion were hoisted above the still-smoking ruins of Fort Sumter, Hannah turned anxiously to Robert.

"What's in store for us?"

It was a question that slaves had been asking all through the winter. Immediately, the war meant trouble, stricter enforcement of slave laws, more patrollers, fewer passes. Fearful of rebellion, planters would no longer permit their slaves to travel from one plantation to another or to visit the city on Sundays. For the first time since he had lived in Charleston, Robert had been unable to return to Beaufort for Christmas.

For free Negroes, matters were almost worse. The legislature was considering laws to confiscate their property and even to sell them back into slavery. When one lawmaker proposed that they be given five dollars as payment for themselves, and the privilege of choosing their own masters, another objected, saying that this was too much privilege. In the month of January, 1861, more than seven hundred free men and women had sold their homes and sailed from Charleston to Haiti or New York.

For a wild moment Robert and Hannah eyed their hoard of greenbacks and thought of joining the flight. But their money was not enough to buy freedom for the three of them and the waterfront was too closely guarded to hope for escape.

Their hope, if there was any hope at all, lay in the future. Eagerly they gathered every scrap of information, puzzling over conversations Hannah overheard at the Mills Hotel, struggling to read through newspapers that Robert brought home. Two great armies were preparing for the field, but what were they fighting for?

The South spoke up boldly. Alexander Stephens, one-time U. S. Congressman, now Vice-President of the Confederate States, explained, "Our new government is founded upon the great truth that the Negro is not equal to the white man, that slavery, subordination to the white race, is his natural and moral condition. This, our new government, is the first in the history of the world based on this great physical, philosophical and moral truth."

The North was not so positive. To be sure, they were fighting for the Union. Yes, they were opposed to slavery in the territories. But abolition? Freeing the slaves of South Carolina? "I have no purpose directly or indirectly to interfere with the institution of slavery in the states where it exists," Abraham Lincoln stated in his inaugural address.

Hannah burst into tears when she heard those words. At election time the planters had declared that Lincoln would free the slaves. Now Lincoln himself said the opposite.

"Just politics." Trying to comfort her, Robert sometimes sounded more confident than he felt. "Besides, what he says don't matter. It's what he does. Suppose a Union army comes to Charleston? All the speeches in the world won't stop the slaves from freeing themselves then."

Suppose a Union army comes to Charleston. The words had a different meaning for the slaves and citizens of the city. While the slaves held secret meetings, pledging themselves to strike for their freedom as soon as they saw a chance of success, the citizens stacked shells on the piers ("anti-abolition pills," they called them), dug trenches on the beaches, and piled up sandbags around the harbor forts. The buoys that marked the ship channels were removed, the lights in the lighthouses turned off, and torpedoes were placed in the nearby rivers.

Along the waterfront there were no longer any ships from Boston and New York, and only an occasional British merchant vessel dared to defy the Union's blockade of the Atlantic coast. As bales of cotton piled up in the warehouses and rotted on the piers, Simmons' yard went on a war footing. For a few months all hands were busy transforming the cotton boats into men-of-war. But this work could not last forever and in July, 1861, Robert shipped on the *Planter* as a deck hand.

The *Planter* was a paddle-wheel steamer owned by Captain John Ferguson and chartered to the Confederate Government for $125 a day. One hundred and

forty feet long and fifty feet wide, she could transport fourteen hundred bales of cotton or one thousand
armed men. One of the fastest ships in the harbor, she
was particularly valuable for river work because her
light draft allowed her to travel in shallow coastal
waters without running aground.

During the summer of 1861, the *Planter* sailed down
the coast, making a survey of Rebel ports all the way
to Florida. Robert was promoted to wheelsman, the
closest a slave could come to being called "pilot" in
the Confederate Navy. Most of his sailing was done in
familiar waters, on the rivers and bays near Beaufort.
He helped to destroy the federal lighthouses on Hunting Island and to lay torpedoes in the Edisto and Stono
Rivers. For this he was paid sixteen dollars a month,
fifteen dollars of which he turned over to Henry McKee.

With Charleston defenses well under way, Rebel
engineers turned their attention to Port Royal harbor.
The *Planter* steamed back and forth from Charleston,
carrying crews of carpenters and masons, lumber,
cannons, soldiers, to the two new forts that were being
built, Fort Beauregard at Bay Point and Fort Walker
at Hilton Head.

As the cotton ripened in the fields and the hot summer gave way to fall's clear cool days there were rumors of a Union fleet assembling at Hampton Roads in
Virginia. Seventy-five gunboats and steamers, frigates
and sailing vessels, the newspapers reported, and an
army of ten thousand men.

Late in October chattering instruments in the telegraph offices confirmed the rumors. The fleet had
cleared the Virginia capes and was traveling south-
ward. But was its destination Charleston, Savannah, or
Port Royal? No one knew.

On November 2, the Charleston *Mercury* warned of the approach of the "Yankee armada." On November 3, the citizens of the city thronged to the waterfront to stare at the plumes of smoke that were visible on the horizon. But the great fleet moved slowly onward to anchor off Port Royal Bay the following day.

While the Union ships sailed along the coast, the *Planter* followed the inland waterways, bringing ammunition and new recruits for the Beaufort Artillery at Fort Beauregard. These were the same troops whose drills Robert had watched at the Arsenal on Craven Street when he was a boy. Now, as they shouted, "Death to the Yankees," he must be careful not to show, even by the twitch of an eyebrow, what he was thinking.

For two days gale winds and rain slowed down the expedition, but when the sun shone on calm seas on the morning of the seventh—a year and a day since Abraham Lincoln's election—both sides knew that the hour had come.

From a safe anchorage in the Beaufort River, Robert watched the battle. Led by the U.S.S. *Wabash*, the Union vessels swept into the harbor. Cannonballs whizzed through the air; flames spurted and dense clouds of smoke rolled up from the water. The guns of the *Wabash* were firing in such rapid succession that for a moment Robert feared that the flagship had caught fire. But it steamed onward, gliding around the harbor in a great circle to aim its guns first at Fort Walker, then at Fort Beauregard.

In Charleston, sixty miles away, Hannah listened anxiously to the booming of the far-off cannon. By mid-afternoon there was silence. The last Rebel guns were emptied. The last gray-clad soldier had left his post and the Stars and Stripes once more snapped in the breeze above Port Royal Bay.

Long before this the *Planter* had fled upriver, stopping at Beaufort to refuel. Even before the boat tied up at the dock, Robert could hear the familiar tones of the jail house bell. Only this time it was calling a curfew for the slaveholders. This time it was warning the masters of the enemy's approach.

At each stroke of the bell, planters and their families swarmed to the piers, pleading for transportation from the city. Overloaded boats steamed up the river and every carriage and cart was pressed into service, jamming the roads to the mainland.

When Union soldiers marched into Beaufort, there was only one white man left in town. And he, according to the New York *World,* "appeared to be paralyzed by drunkenness or fear, and it probably was not the latter. He met the Federal troops on the outskirts of the city and with hat in hand, and gently swaying from side to side, hiccuped out a few indistinguishable words as they passed."

It was different with the slaves. As the panicked planters fled in one direction, their "articles of merchandise" traveled in the other. Before the clouds of smoke had lifted from Port Royal Bay there were Negroes at the waterfront begging to be taken aboard the Union boats and offering to guide the soldiers to Rebel Army headquarters.

Week after week they continued to come, at first from the nearby islands, then from plantations up the rivers and from the Georgia and Florida coasts. In one day, seven thousand of them arrived in Beaufort, traveling in bateaus, dugout canoes and on homemade rafts with a blanket for a sail. Young women with babies on their backs, boys and girls of all sizes and colors, old people and able-bodied men—came to meet "the Lincoln soldiers."

After the battle of Port Royal, when Robert visited the Ancrums to turn over his monthly pay, he found the McKee family there, refugees from Beaufort.

"Don't know what came over Lydia," Henry McKee grumbled. "Day after the battle she helped us pack and then up and disappeared. Woman her age ought to of had more sense. We were counting on her to come with us. Mistress needs her."

Robert clucked sympathetically, trying to look concerned about his mother and his mistress. But he knew what had come over Lydia. At the age of seventy-one she was free!

Or almost free. It wasn't long before the grapevine telegraph was carrying messages to Charleston from Union South Carolina and the Smalls learned of a new word—"contraband." The word had been coined by General Benjamin Butler, commander at Fortress Monroe, when the slaves of Virginia flocked to his lines. Since the Union was not in the business of freeing slaves Army officers had courteously returned runaways to their rebellious masters. But Butler decided on a different policy. The slaves had been raising food and working on fortifications for their masters. Butler declared them enemy property—"contraband of war"—and put them to work for the Union. "Contraband" meant not slave, but not quite free or human either.

At Port Royal the contrabands went to work with a will, transforming Hilton Head into a naval base with wharves and coal yards, repair shops and ammunition depots for the ships of the South Atlantic Blockading

Squadron. Beaufort became the headquarters of the Army, the military capital of Union South Carolina, known as the Department of the South. Able-bodied contrabands worked as laborers on the wharves, as carpenters and masons, cooks, laundresses, spies and scouts.

But there were many others, old people, the sick, the children, who needed help in order to live in freedom. In the North abolitionists and church groups, Negro and white, organized sewing circles and aid societies. They filled "contraband boxes" with dresses, shoes, medicines, and sent teachers, slates and books to the Department of the South. Government agents in Beaufort hired contrabands to farm the abandoned plantations. By the spring of 1862, the first crop of "free cotton" was being planted on Lady's Island and thousands of black-skinned pupils were learning their ABCs from the lady teachers of the North.

When a Beaufort contraband slipped through the enemy's lines to visit his family in Charleston, he brought word from Lydia. She was well and happy, living in her old room and cooking for the Union soldiers who had moved into the McKees' empty house. On Lady's Island, she reported, the Ashdale field hands were working for the government and had been promised a school for their children.

In an answering message by the grapevine telegraph, Robert informed her that she now had a grandson, Robert, Jr. "Tell her love from the four of us and we'll see her soon."

We heard words of hope even amid the din of battle and the clash of arms. We began to realize that we were human beings.

Robert Smalls

7. A Dream Becomes a Plan

The months that followed the fall of Port Royal were busy ones for Robert. The *Planter* had become the flagship and dispatch boat of General Roswell Ripley, second-in-command of Charleston's defenses. As he piloted the ship to the harbor forts, Robert learned the location of every torpedo and obstruction in the channels and of every camouflaged battery on the palmetto-fringed beaches of the islands. He knew the strength of each fort—and its weakness.

All that winter, while he was helping to fortify Charleston against attack, he was struggling with an idea. Perhaps it first came to him when he heard from Lydia. Perhaps it was when he looked through the captain's field glasses at the Union fleet anchored just beyond the bar. Or when the newspapers reported that Congress had abolished slavery in Washington.

The idea was a simple one. There was freedom in Beaufort, in Washington. There was freedom just beyond the bar, seven miles away. Instead of waiting until freedom came to him, he could travel out to meet it.

As he listened to General Ripley talk over defense plans with Captain Relyea, the *Planter*'s captain, his idea grew more complicated. He possessed much useful information and could acquire more. Freedom for himself, freedom for Hannah and the children, yes. But he must also strike a blow that would help the Union win the war.

Night after night, Robert and Hannah discussed and discarded plans. Maybe they could travel by land and river to Beaufort, using their savings to bribe ferrymen and patrollers until they reached the Union lines. Maybe the *Planter*'s slave crew could overpower the three white officers and sail the boat to the Union fleet.

"And leave the children and me in Charleston," Hannah pointed out.

When they finally arrived at a solution it was so simple that Robert wondered why he hadn't thought of it before. It started with Captain Relyea's hat, the broad-brimmed straw hat that he wore to protect his eyes from the glare of the sun on the water. The officers had gone ashore for the night and the crew were talking together in the pilot-house.

"Just fooling around," Robert explained to Hannah. "Alfred Gridiron—he's the fireman—put Relyea's hat on my head. I walked around with my arms folded across my chest the way he does. And then——" He paused as if he had something important to say.

"And then?" Hannah prompted him.

"They all laughed."

"They laughed?" She was disappointed.

"Don't you see?" Robert grabbed her hand. "They laughed because I looked so much like the captain."

It was true, Hannah thought. Both men were short and strongly built. Except for their skin color, they did look alike. But what difference did it make?

"All the difference in the world," Robert assured her. "The difference between slavery and freedom. One night when the officers are on shore, we're going to take the boat. Put you and the children aboard and sail it out to the bar. With me wearing Relyea's hat, the sentries'll think it's him and let us pass. It's very simple."

It was daringly simple, dangerously simple.

"And what'll happen if you're caught?" Hannah asked.

"I'll be shot." Robert spoke soberly. "Sure it's a risk. But freedom's only seven miles away. Freedom for Elizabeth, for Robert."

Hannah was silent, thoughtful. Then, "I'll go," she decided. "Where you die, I'll die."

On a Sunday afternoon in April the crew of the *Planter* met in the Smalls' rooms on East Bay Street. Swearing them to secrecy, Robert explained his plan. The women and children—there would be five women and three youngsters—would be hidden on a merchant ship in the Cooper River. Under cover of darkness the *Planter* would sail up the river and take them aboard. Then Robert would head for the Union blockading fleet beyond the bar.

One by one he answered their objections until his confidence won them over. There was still one matter left to be settled. Suppose they were caught? Suppose a sentry gave the alarm? Suppose they were stopped at Fort Johnson or at Sumter?

All eyes turned to Robert. "Then we scuttle the ship to keep it from the Rebels. If it doesn't sink fast enough to keep us from being captured, we take hold of each other's hands and jump overboard."

The silence was heavy in the little room as they thought over the meaning of his words. A chair squeaked and someone coughed nervously. Then there was a slow nodding of heads.

"It's good weather for swimming. Water in the harbor's getting warm," Jebel Turner cheerfully announced, and the tension in the room turned to laughter.

The next weeks were anxious ones. The decision about the date of departure had been left up to Robert and he refused to be hurried.

"No use going empty-handed," he explained. "There's some new plan they're talking about at headquarters. I aim to find out what it is before we start."

Daily he eavesdropped on the captain's conversations. General Ripley was shortening his defense lines. General Ripley expected a Union attack through the main ship channel. General Ripley was stripping his defenses along the inland waterways and placing all available guns and men in the harbor forts.

Then came the day when the *Planter* was ordered to Cole's Island at the mouth of the Stono River, to move guns from there to Fort Ripley.

"Removing the batteries on Cole's Island?" Smith, the mate, questioned the order. "With those batteries gone, the river's wide open for an enemy attack. And the Stono River's the back door to Charleston."

Robert stared straight ahead, pretending not to hear the conversation. Everyone in Charleston knew that the British had captured the city during the Revolution by sailing their fleet up the Stono River and bypassing the harbor forts.

When Smith pointed this out, Captain Relyea only

shrugged his shoulders. "The General orders us to Cole's Island to remove the guns," he repeated.

"Yes, sir." As Smith saluted and left the pilot-house Robert's heart skipped a beat. This was the information he had been waiting for. The *Planter* would help to open the back door to Charleston—and then the *Planter* would invite the Union to come in.

For the next two days the *Planter* anchored off Cole's Island while her crew dismantled the batteries and moved the guns to the dock. On Sunday when she returned to Charleston, Robert asked for a few hours' leave.

"My little boy's been sick," he explained, "and I'm anxious after him."

"You know the orders, Bob," the captain reminded him. "Officers and crew to remain on board day and night, even in the harbor."

Robert knew the orders. He also knew that the officers often disregarded them and were, in fact, planning to attend a party ashore the following evening. But all that he replied was, "Yes, sir."

Relyea considered the problem further. Robert was a good pilot, a steady man. "All right," he agreed. "But be sure to report back by five o'clock."

"Aye, aye, sir. Thank you, sir." Robert's voice betrayed nothing of the excitement that was bubbling inside him.

Taking his leave of the crew, he walked along the Battery toward his home, pausing at Atlantic Wharf to see which merchant vessels were tied up there. When he turned in at the stable on East Bay Street, his footsteps quickened and he took the stairs two at a time. A glance at his face told Hannah the news.

"Tomorrow."

Briefly he outlined the plan. Tomorrow evening she was to take the children and board the *Etowan* at Atlantic Wharf. Members of the crew would hide them until the *Planter* pulled up alongside.

"Tomorrow." He traveled through the city bringing the message to the other women, making arrangements with the steward of the *Etowan.*

"Tomorrow." Even Elizabeth, catching the mood of her parents, repeated the word when he returned home. He held her on his lap, rumpling her hair, as he went over last-minute details with Hannah. Nothing must be forgotten.

Hanna᾽., too, had news. The Charleston papers said that General Hunter, commander of the Department of the South, was freeing the slaves all along the coast. "The persons in these three states, Georgia, Florida and South Carolina, heretofore held as slaves," his proclamation announced, "are therefore declared forever free."

Forever free! Robert's face lit up. The contrabands would become freedmen, citizens. With Hunter's proclamation and Ripley's new defense plan, surely now was the time to strike.

Walking back to the wharf, past Ryan's jail and the Planters Hotel, he took his last look at Charleston. In front of the slave mart on Chalmers Street there was a poster advertising "Prime Negroes for Sale."

Business as usual—but the city had changed greatly since the beginning of the war. A fire had destroyed many of the familiar landmarks, including St. Andrew's Hall, where the articles of secession had been written. The Battery was deserted except for pacing sentries and White Point Gardens was a regimental camp ground, brightened with tents by day and campfires at night. King Street, which had once seemed so grand to a small boy from Beaufort, was empty, its shop windows laid bare by the Union blockade.

Coffee, Hannah told him, cost $1.50 a pound and was almost unobtainable. So was wool. One of her ladies at the Mills Hotel had knitted a pair of socks for Jefferson Davis, writing to explain that they were made from the clipped curls of her pet lap dog. Hannah's story reminded Robert of a joke that was making the rounds of the harbor boats. There was so little salt in the South, the sailors solemnly declared, that all good Rebels were scolding their wives and spanking their children as a patriotic duty, so that they would shed briny tears into the beef and pork barrels!

The bells of St. Michael's were striking five when Robert entered the crew's quarters of the *Planter* with a laundry bag slung over his shoulder. A bag containing a surprising number of children's shirts and dresses and Hannah's best white sheet, which was to serve as a flag of truce.

Early the next morning the *Planter* headed down the Stono for her last trip to Cole's Island. "All guns to be aboard by noon and delivered to Fort Ripley before dark," the captain commanded.

The captain commanded, but the crew decided otherwise. Perhaps it was because the weather was unseasonably warm for May. Perhaps the men had eaten something that disagreed with them. Whatever the reason, Captain Relyea had never seen them work so slowly or so carelessly.

Ropes that should have been fastened came untied. Lines slipped through fumbling hands. Twice the block and tackle crashed to the deck and a cannon almost fell into the river. When John dropped a board on

Abram's foot all hands left their tasks to see the damage and to give advice to the limping man.

By noon, only one gun had been moved aboard. The captain was purple with rage, the men polite and regretful. Robert could hardly keep a straight face as he listened to the cheerful chorus of "Aye, aye," that greeted Relyea's bellowed orders.

It was not until four in the afternoon, too late for the trip to Fort Ripley that day, that the remainder of the arms were made fast on the deck of the *Planter*. There were a 7-inch rifle and four cannons, one of them a cannon belonging to Fort Sumter that had been damaged during the Rebel attack and recently repaired. Robert checked its moorings carefully. Now there must be no slack lines or slipping knots. He intended to return this cannon to its rightful owner.

As soon as the *Planter* tied up at Southern Wharf, Relyea and his officers went ashore. There was a party that night at Fort Sumter, a ball given by the ladies of Charleston for their city's gallant defenders. There would be dancing on the moonlit parade ground and a round of toasts to President Davis and the others.

"Mind you take on fuel for an early start in the morning," the captain ordered. "And mind you work properly tomorrow or I'll send the lot of you to Ryan's for a whipping."

"Aye aye, sir," Robert answered for the crew. "We'll be ready for an early start in the morning."

What ship is that a sailing . . .
Negro spiritual

8. A Boy Becomes a Man

There were twenty cords of wood stacked in the engine
room when the sentry guarding General Ripley's headquarters fifty yards away from Southern Wharf sing-
songed:

"Ten o'clock and all's well."

The tides were checked, the signals studied and for
the tenth time Robert rehearsed the plan with the
crew.

"Eleven o'clock and all's well."

Faint sounds drifted across the harbor from Fort
Sumter. The regimental band of the First South Caro-
lina Artillery was playing "Dixie," "Nellie Gray,"
"In the Gloaming." Then came the strains of "Auld
Lang Syne." It was midnight and the ball was over.
Soon the *Marion,* the *Planter*'s sister ship, tied up at the
dock to discharge a boatload of merrymakers. Once
more the waterfront was quiet.

"One o'clock and all's well."

By the light of the moon, Robert and Alfred broke
into the captain's cabin. When they returned to the

crew's quarters they had revolvers in their pockets and muskets under their arms. Robert, wearing Relyea's gold-trimmed jacket, imitated the captain's walk as he distributed the guns. The men laughed nervously.

"This waiting sure is hard," William Morrison murmured. "When do we start?"

"Soon. You can write, can't you, Will?" Robert asked.

Morrison nodded.

"Here's the ship's log. Keep it just like the mate does. Put down our names, when we start and all, like on a regular trip."

Will leafed through the logbook, glad of something to occupy his mind. Alfred and John left to light the fires while Jebel and Sam stood on deck, ready to cast off.

It was three o'clock on the morning of May 13, 1862, when Alfred reported a full head of steam in the boilers. In the bow, Jebel quietly cut the moorings of the boat, using strings to lower the cables into the water so that no splash would arouse the sentry. At the stern, Sam hoisted the palmetto flag and the Stars and Bars to the top of the flagstaff.

Robert backed the *Planter* out of her berth alongside the *Marion* and headed upriver. On shore the sentry reported:

"All's well."

Dropping anchor close to the *Etowan,* Robert sent a small boat for the women. The muffled oars scarcely rippled the dark waters of the river. In a quarter hour, the boat headed back with its precious human cargo. From the window of the pilot-house, Robert stared at the straining backs of the oarsmen. In the dim light before the dawn he couldn't make out Hannah's face. But she was there, he knew, with the baby in her arms and Elizabeth at her side. Soon they were aboard—five women, three children and the steward of the *Etowan*, who had decided to cast his lot with the Union, too.

There was no time for greetings. As Jebel led them to the hold, Robert swung the wheel around, turning the ship until her bow pointed toward the sea.

"We leave Charleston at one-half past 3 o'clock on Tuesday morning," Will wrote in the log.

Slowly the ship glided through the waters of the harbor, past Castle Pinckney, abreast of Fort Johnson. Robert leaned forward, pulling the cord of the steam whistle to give the salute. The sentry at the fort wondered what the *Planter* was about so early in the morning. But there was nothing unusual in her movements and he waved his cap as she went by.

They had passed Fort Johnson, passed Fort Moultrie, when Alfred appeared at Robert's side, grimy and worried.

"Sumter's next. Let's put on steam and sail by fast, without stopping," he suggested.

"And have every gun at the fort trained on us, ready to blow us out of the water?" Robert had thought this through many times before. "No, we'll take it nice and easy, like always."

Alfred sighed. Robert was right, but the suspense was almost more than a man could bear. As he returned to the engine room, Robert peered through the captain's field glasses. There was Fort Sumter, enormous, forbidding, and almost dead ahead.

Three miles beyond, just visible in the first rays of the morning sun, were the ships of the Union fleet. A flag was slowly traveling to the top of a mast and Robert thought he could hear a bugle playing reveille.

Now the *Planter* was within hailing distance of Fort Sumter. The engines throbbed, the paddle wheels cut through the water, but a dead silence blanketed the men on the ship. Even the children below decks were quiet. Suppose the sentry insisted on speaking to one of the officers? Suppose there was a new order to be given, a question asked?

Turning the wheel over to Sam, Robert leaned on the window sill of the pilot-house with his arms folded across his chest and Captain Relyea's broad-brimmed straw hat shadowing his face. He stared into the muzzles of Sumter's guns as he raised his hand for the signal cord.

One, two, three short blasts on the steam whistle, then a long hissing sound.

He could hear Sam's breathing and the screeching of the gulls overhead. After a moment that seemed like an hour there was a shout from the sentinel on the parapet:

"Corporal of the guard, the *Planter,* flagship for General Ripley, giving the prescribed signal with her whistle."

"Pass the *Planter,* flagship for General Ripley," the guard replied.

Pass the *Planter!* Never had ordinary words sounded so sweet. The morning sun shone with a special brightness and in the hold Hannah began to croon a song to her baby.

As the boat steamed by the fort, the gray-clad sentry called across the water, "Blow the damned Yankees to hell or bring one of them in."

"Aye, aye, sir." Robert smiled as he answered.

In the crew's quarters Will leaned on a sea chest to scrawl, "We pass Fort Sumter one-quarter past 4 o'clock." Three more miles to go.

The *Planter* continued her leisurely pace until she was outside the range of Sumter's guns. Then Robert signalled for more steam and the ship leaped ahead, ploughing through the water. Puzzled by her burst of speed, the lookout on Sumter's high wall followed her course through his glasses. He watched her pass Morris Island and continue out to sea.

Something was wrong. Calling to the corporal of the guard, he gave the alarm. Signals flashed—from Sumter to Morris Island, from Sumter to Charleston—but it was too late to stop the *Planter*.

The ship was now in no man's land, between the two opposing forces. As they neared the bar, Robert ordered the Rebel flags lowered and the bedsheet flag of truce run up to the top of the foremast.

He steered for the U.S.S. *Onward,* the forward ship of the Union fleet. They were near enough now to hear the beating of drums on the Union vessel. The beating of drums! Robert's heart sank. The drums were a signal for all hands to make ready for the enemy.

The *Onward* was turning, her cannon trained on the *Planter* and her open portholes bristling with guns. In the morning mist her officers had failed to see the white flag of truce.

Robert's hands tightened on the spokes of the wheel. Had he brought the ship this far, only to be fired on by Union men? Leaning hard on the wheel, he swung the *Planter* around, hoping to pass the *Onward*'s bow, and continued his seaward course.

As the *Planter* turned, heading into the wind, the limp bedsheet on her mast caught the ocean breeze and billowed outward. Staring at the flapping sheet, the Union commander ordered his men to hold their fire.

"Ahoy there, what steamer is that?" he shouted. "State your business."

"The *Planter*, out of Charleston," Robert bellowed. "Come to join the Union fleet."

There was a moment of stunned silence. Then a command floated across the water. "Pull alongside. But keep your men away from the guns or I'll blow you to bits."

Five minutes later, the *Planter* had dropped anchor next to the *Onward* and an astonished Union officer was climbing aboard the Confederate ship. Robert left the pilot-house to salute him.

"I have the honor, sir, to present the *Planter*, formerly the flagship of General Ripley. In addition to her own armament, she carries four cannon which were to have been delivered to Fort Ripley this morning. I thought they might be of some service to Uncle Abe."

It was spoken with dignity and assurance, the dignity of a boy who has just become a man.

As the *Planter*'s crew stood at attention, the white flag was lowered and the Stars and Stripes raised in its place. In the log Will noted, "We arrive at blockading squadron at Charleston Bar at a quarter to 6. We give three cheers for the Union flag once more."

*Our community was intensely agitated on Tuesday
morning by the intelligence that the steamer* Planter
*had been taken possession of by her colored crew and
boldly run out to the blockaders. The news at first
was not credited.*

Charleston *Courier*, May 14, 1862.

9. At Charleston's Back Door

It was hard to keep track of everything that happened
in the next few days. From the *Planter,* Robert was
rowed to the *Augusta* to talk with Commander Parrott, senior officer of the blockading squadron. Parott
greeted him courteously, listening to his account of the
trip and glancing at the Charleston newspapers that he
brought with him.

"Now about those guns you have aboard. They
were to have been delivered this morning to the new
fort on the middle ground?"

"Yes, sir." Robert nodded. "But the important thing's
where they came from. Ripley's stripping his defenses
along the Stono in order to concentrate his fire power
in the harbor proper. He expects you to attack from
here. Instead, if you go up the Stono . . ."

He talked on, describing the dismantled batteries

on Cole's Island, the narrow entrance to the river, the history of the British invasion of the city.

With lifted eyebrows, Parrott interrupted to ask question after question. Robert had questions too, about himself and his crew, Hannah and the children. Were they contrabands, freedmen, citizens? And what was to be done with the *Planter?* He knew that an enemy ship seized in wartime was a prize of war and that its captors were awarded prize money, according to the value of the vessel. Would this law apply when the captors were slaves?

But his questions must wait. Parrott was writing to Commander du Pont at Port Royal. "I have the honor to inform you that the rebel armed steamer *Planter* was brought out to us this morning from Charleston by eight contrabands. I send her to Port Royal at once, in order to take advantage of the present good weather. I send Charleston papers of the 12th, and the very intelligent contraband who was in charge will give you the information which he has brought off."

Before noon, the *Planter* set out for Port Royal, with an officer and five sailors from the *Augusta* aboard. Steaming through the familiar waters of St. Helena Sound, rounding the bend that led from the Coosaw River to the Beaufort, Robert felt as if his heart would burst with joy. He wanted to sing, to set off rockets and ring bells.

Elizabeth slipped away from Hannah and made her way to the pilot-house to find him.

"Where we going, Poppa?" she asked.

Giving the wheel to one of the Union sailors, he picked her up and carried her out on deck. As they passed Beaufort the soldiers and civilians working on the wharves paused to gape at the Rebel ship that was flying the Union flag.

Robert pointed out the sights to Elizabeth, the places where he'd swum and fished as a boy, the ferry that went to Lady's Island. Through the tops of the trees he thought he could see the chimneys of the house on Prince Street.

"You're home, Lizzie, home. Tomorrow, you'll see your grandma."

It was ten o'clock at night and Elizabeth was asleep in her father's hammock when the *Planter* tied up at the new wharf at Hilton Head. A rowboat carried Robert to the *Wabash*. Climbing up the ship's ladder, he thought back to the battle of Port Royal, six months earlier, and felt as if he were dreaming.

But Samuel du Pont was a real, in-the-flesh naval commander with gold epaulettes on his shoulders and gold stripes on the sleeves of his coat. Brusque, businesslike, he too fired questions at Robert.

Robert answered gravely, forgetting both the gold braid and his own problems in the business at hand. When he had finished, Du Pont rose to pace his cabin.

"If you're right, young man, the Rebels have committed a great military error by abandoning their Stono defenses. If you're right——" Abruptly he began to make notes, give orders.

"The *Planter* will return to Beaufort with its crew and their families. They'll be taken care of." He turned to Robert. "But you'll stay here. I want you to lead a squadron to the Stono."

"To attack Charleston?" Robert's face was wreathed in smiles.

"No, man, no. First to scout the enemy's position.

73

Then—we'll see." Du Pont's wave of the hand was a gesture of dismissal.

After Robert left his cabin, the commander dictated a report to Gideon Welles, Secretary of the Navy, in Washington.

". . . The bringing out of this steamer, under all the circumstances, would have done credit to anyone. The armament of the steamer is a 32-pounder, on pivot, and a fine 24-pound howitzer. She had, besides, on her deck, four other guns, one 7-inch rifle, which were to be taken on the morning of the escape to the new fort on the middle ground. One of the four belonged to Fort Sumter, and had been struck, in the rebel attack on that fort, on the muzzle.

"Robert, the intelligent slave and pilot of the boat, who performed this bold feat so skillfully, informed me of this fact, presuming it would be a matter of interest to us to have possession of this gun.

"This man, Robert Smalls, is superior to any who has yet come into the lines, intelligent as many of them have been. His information has been most interesting, and portions of it of the utmost importance.

"The steamer is quite a valuable acquisition to the squadron, by her good machinery and very light draft.

"I do not know whether, in the views of the Government, the vessel will be considered a prize; but, if so, I respectfully submit to the Department the claims of this man Robert and his associates."

There was time for only a few hours' sleep and the briefest of farewells to his family before the *Planter* left for Beaufort and Robert was escorted to headquarters at Hilton Head. All day long he retold the story of the capture of the *Planter,* to General Benham and his aides, and then to the newspaper reporters.

In a week's time, Robert Smalls was a celebrity, a national hero. All over the North, newspapers praised his deed.

"One of the most daring and heroic adventures since the war commenced . . . A gallant feat . . . a good blow struck in our behalf by the black loyalists of South Carolina."

"If we must still remember with humility that the Confederate flag yet waves where our national colors were first struck, we should be all the more prompt to recognize the merit that has put into our possession the first trophy from Fort Sumter . . . A slave has brought away from under the very guns of the enemy, where no fleet of ours has yet dared to venture, a prize whose possession a commodore thinks worthy to be announced in a special dispatch."

Harper's Weekly published his photograph, alongside a picture of the *Planter,* and the Count of Paris, reporting the Civil War for French audiences, wrote of the "remarkable incident" and the "daring and intelligent Negro" who carried it out. There was even one imaginative correspondent who described Robert as "a very ancient old darky" who said, "I was born under the old flag and I'se getting old, and I jist feel as though I'd like to die under it."

The twenty-three-year old pilot knew nothing of his sudden rise to fame. On the twentieth of May he led three Union gunboats across the bar that marked the entrance of the Stono River. They steamed past Cole's Island to make a landing at Legareville, on the river's western shore. Finding Robert's information correct, other gunboats followed to occupy the Rebels' abandoned forts and make prisoners of their pickets.

By the end of the month, Du Pont was writing to

Secretary Welles: "I have the honor to inform the Department that the gunboats have possession of Stono. From information derived chiefly from the contraband pilot, Robert Smalls, I had reason to believe that the rebels had abandoned their batteries. We are in as complete possession of the river as of Port Royal, and can land and protect the army whenever it wishes."

In Beaufort, the Army was making plans for a full-scale attack. Daily, General Hunter pleaded with Washington for soldiers and boats to transport them. "With the necessary steamers and a few thousand additional troops, we could soon have Charleston," he reported.

Slowly, too slowly, Robert thought, the Union built up its strength along the Stono. By the first week in June, there were three thousand soldiers in camps on James Island, only five miles from Charleston. As soon as more troops arrived they would advance across the island to Fort Johnson. With Fort Johnson in their hands, the Union would control Charleston harbor.

It was a fine plan. Robert, who had pored over maps with the generals, pointing out the location of enemy batteries, explaining where troops could travel along the creeks and across the marshes, heartily approved of it. It was a fine plan, if the troops arrived, if ships were sent to transport them, if the enemy was not given time to rebuild his defenses.

Returning to the *Planter,* Robert piloted her from the North Edisto River to James Island, delivering companies of soldiers and their baggage. The ship landed troops, cavalry, ambulance wagons along the creeks, in waters too shallow for the big Navy vessels. Impatiently, its pilot buttonholed anyone who would listen, to urge the need for speed and to beg to be allowed to take part when the big attack came.

"I wish to the good Lord when they got to Charleston, they would let me go along," he told a reporter. "I would like to fight against Charleston, even if I should die for it."

Had he been in Charleston at that moment he would certainly have died. Within hours of the *Planter*'s departure from the city Rebel telegraph wires were buzzing with the news. From Charleston to Savannah, from Savannah to Richmond, the word traveled:

"The steamer *Planter*, with five guns aboard, intended for the harbor, was stolen in Charleston this morning."

General Robert E. Lee wired orders "to bring to punishment any party or parties that may be proved guilty of complicity in the affair or negligent in not preventing it." A Savannah newspaper suggested that the military be put in petticoats for permitting "this extraordinary occurrence" and the Charleston *Mercury* pleaded for mercy for "the late captain, mate and engineer of the Steamer *Planter*."

At first the Rebels were embarrassed by the daring exploit of these "beings of an inferior order." But their embarrassment turned to genuine alarm when from the Battery they could hear the Union's guns along the Stono. General Ripley was ordered to "suspend all other work until the Stono is thoroughly obstructed, as it is essential that the work should be done at once, and it will be prosecuted day and night until finished."

As weeks went by, the Rebels had ample time to realize their mistakes and correct them. Rafts of heavy timbers strapped with iron were anchored in the river. New batteries were built along the banks and troops transferred there from the harbor forts. The element of surprise that Robert had counted on for a quick Union victory no longer existed. The Union could win now only by bringing in troops and more troops until they overwhelmed the defenders of Charleston.

But the troops never came. On the sixteenth of June, disobeying General Hunter's order not to advance without reinforcements, General Benham led an attack. Outnumbered by the Rebels, he retreated six hours later, leaving six hundred dead men on the marshes of James Island. Benham was arrested and sent North to face a court-martial while on the *Planter*, Robert helped to evacuate the soldiers he had ferried to the island a short time before.

Eight weeks after the *Planter* had been captured, eight weeks after Robert had pointed out the road to Charleston's back door, there were no Union soldiers left on James Island. The back door was closed and in Beaufort a reporter warned his editor, "Do not expect the fall of Charleston too speedily."

*Our people want to know if they fight for the Union
if they get liberty or be slaves. If they be free they
will all fight.*

Port Royal contraband, 1862

10. Better Than Slavery

For Robert, the failure of the James Island expedition
was a bitter disappointment. It was hard to understand
the reasons for delay—if there were reasons—hard to
forgive the disobedience of orders, hard to forget the
dead men on the marshes. He was too young, too new
in this white man's world, to shrug his shoulders and
dismiss the matter calmly.

"They say there's no more troops to be had. They're
all needed for McClellan in Virginia." He was talking
to Alfred Gridiron on the deck of the *Planter* one
night. The two were shipmates again, stationed in the
North Edisto River. "But if they'd arm the Negroes,
make soldiers out of the contrabands——"

Alfred sighed. He had heard Robert say this before.
"But there's nothing you can do about it."

"Not now, maybe," Robert agreed. "But when I get
shore leave I'm sure going to try to get some action."

"You're getting plenty of action here," Alfred

teased. "Didn't I see you duck when those Reb shells bounced off the pilot-house today?"

"How could you see me duck when you were hiding in the engine room?" Robert retorted.

Despite their joking, both men were proud of the way they had been standing up under enemy fire. For the *Planter* was now a gunboat in the U. S. Navy. Lieutenant Rhind, in charge of operations on the North Edisto, had built musket-proof bulwarks on her deck and had hired a crew of contrabands to furnish wood for her boilers. Because of her ability to navigate in the tidal bays and creeks, he used her to lead attacks on Rebel outposts many miles inland.

On today's expedition Robert had piloted the *Planter,* followed by Rhind on the *Crusader,* through Wadmalaw Sound and as far as Simmon's Bluff on the mainland. When the boats passed the bluff, Rebel sharpshooters concealed in rifle pits along the shore let loose a volley of shots. From the pilot-house, Robert watched the union gunners load and fire, load and fire, until the enemy fled to the woods. Then he brought the *Planter* into shore and a company of soldiers scrambled up the bank to set fire to the Rebel camp and collect the muskets they had left behind.

"We returned to our anchorage off the wharf about 6 PM," Lieutenant Rhind wrote to Commander du Pont, "without loss and with very trifling damage."

There had been other trips along the rivers, with Robert pointing out torpedoes that he had helped to put in place the year before, other engagements with the enemy at Rockville, off John's Island and at Adam's Run. By the time he returned to Beaufort for his first shore leave, he felt like a seasoned veteran.

But a veteran without title or pay. The contrabands

who cut wood for the *Planter*'s boilers were paid two
dollars a cord. The ex-slaves building wharves and
warehouses at Hilton Head received eight dollars a
month in U.S. greenbacks. Smalls, pilot of a gunboat
which he had given to the Union, was something of
a problem. On the face of it, he was entitled to the
same pay as a white man and to officer's rank. But—
and here everyone he spoke to became uncomfortable
—there were such things as regulations and tradition.

"The navy's strong on tradition," people said. "Never had a colored officer. As for regulations, have you
seen Secretary Welles' last order? Contrabands can
be enlisted, but they're to be rated as 'boys,' with pay
of from eight to ten dollars a month."

"A boy again." Robert smiled ruefully at he talked
with Hannah and Lydia. "Seems as if I'll never grow
up, even though I'm free. Or am I free?"

There was some question about that too. President
Lincoln had disapproved of General Hunter's proclamation of freedom for the Department of the South,
declaring that Hunter was "a little too previous."

"But tell him about Mr. Lovejoy," Lydia interrupted. "Show him all the papers, Hannah."

From a shelf above their heads, Hannah carefully
lifted down a stack of newspapers, all of them containing articles about Smalls and the *Planter*. Owen Lovejoy, whose brother, Elijah, had been shot by a pro-
slavery mob in Illinois twenty-five years earlier, had
introduced a resolution in Congress for the emancipation of Robert Smalls and his fellow crew members.

"Did they vote it?" Robert asked.

"No." Hannah shook her head. "But they passed another law this summer. Mr. Lovejoy made a speech
about it at a meeting in New York."

Robert watched his wife search through the pile of newspapers. "You been learning to read?"

"A little. Go to school some at night. But mostly I know these articles about you by heart. Here's Mr. Lovejoy."

". . . It is only by the law of Congress liberating slaves actually employed in the rebellion that this Robert Smalls is capable of legally owning anything, even himself or the prize money he so fairly earned. I would like to know if those who are in favor of reconstructing slavery back to its former ascendancy are also in favor of taking Robert Smalls and chucking him back under the cowskin of the rebel knave who used to work him for nothing?"

"Rebel knave," Lydia chuckled. "Wonder how Henry McKee likes that."

"Never mind McKee." Robert smiled too. "What's all this about the prize money?"

"You didn't hear about that? Why, that's the best of all." Both women were delighted.

Hannah searched through her treasure trove of papers again. On May 19, Senator James Grimes had asked the Senate to pass a bill "for the benefit of Robert Smalls and others." The *Planter*'s crew was to receive one half of the value of the boat they had captured. The same bill was introduced into the House by Elihu Washburne of Illinois, a close friend of the President's. During the House vote, Congressman Crittenden, a slave owner from the Border State of Kentucky took his hat and his departure, followed by other Kentucky members. Despite their absence, the bill passed and on the thirty-first of May it was signed by Abraham Lincoln.

"And here's a copy of the bill itself." With Hannah's help, Robert made his way through the fine print:

"Be it enacted by the Senate and House of Representatives of the United States of America in Congress assembled . . ."

"Have you heard how much they say the *Planter*'s worth?" he asked.

"That's here too. Commander du Pont sent you a copy of his letter to Secretary Welles." Hannah was beaming as she watched Robert study the figures in the report.

He went over them again, not sure that he had deciphered them correctly. "It says here, 'Value of the vessel and her armament, $9,000. Value of loose guns $168. Total, $9,168.' Is that what you make it?"

Hannah nodded. "And you'll get fifteen hundred dollars as the leader of the party. Isn't it wonderful? We've been making so many plans."

"Fifteen hundred dollars," Lydia repeated. "The price of a prime field hand. Wonder what Henry McKee'll think of *that*."

Robert didn't know what to say. It was wonderful and yet it wasn't. Fifteen hundred dollars would feed and clothe his family for years. It would buy them a house so that they could move from the old slave quarters in which they were living.

"But it's wrong," he explained. "If we'd been white men we'd get the full value of the *Planter*, not just half. Do you know what the *Planter*'s really worth?"

Crestfallen, Hannah and Lydia shook their heads.

"Mr. Baldwin—he's captain of the *Mercury*, a steam tug that the Navy charters—looked her over when we got to Hilton Head. He said she's a first-class steamboat,

83

worth $75,000 for the boat alone. And that's not fig-
uring the cannon."

"The loose guns were sent to New York to be valued," Hannah informed him.

"And look at the price they put on them. One hundred and sixty-eight dollars," Robert exploded. "Why,
the cannon from Fort Sumter alone cost the Rebels
more than that to repair. And there was hundreds of
shells and rifle charges aboard. Alfred and I figured
out, counting cannon and powder, that we'd brought
off seven thousand dollars' worth of guns and ammunition. At prices the way they were before the war. It'd
be more now."

For a few minutes nobody spoke. Lydia was thinking, thinking back over her seventy-one years in
slavery and the few short months she had spent as a
free woman.

"You got no cause to be upset, Son," she finally
concluded. "It's wrong, unfair. But it's better than
slavery, a whole heap better. It takes time to make
big changes and we're only at the beginning. They've
got a lot to learn—and so, Good Lord, do we."

Hannah was close to tears. She'd been looking forward to Robert's return so she could share the good
news with him. Now, instead of being happy, he was
angry. He was right, of course, but——

"You didn't take the *Planter* for the prize money,"
she reminded him, "and things are better here than
in Charleston. Today, General Hunter stopped me on
the street. Said he'd like to see you soon's you got back.
He called me 'Mrs. Smalls.' First time a white man's
ever called me anything but 'Hannah' or 'gal.'"

Robert's face brightened. He'd been hearing about
General Hunter. "Black Dave," as his soldiers called

him, was a regular army man who had been part of Lincoln's military escort when the President-Elect traveled from Springfield to Washington. After the inauguration, Hunter commanded the Frontier Guards who patrolled the White House. Later, he had been wounded at Bull Run and had served in the West.

Ever since March, when he'd taken over the command of the Department of the South, he'd given the War Department no rest. In addition to his proclamation of freedom for the slaves, he badgered Washington with demands for more troops. When they failed to arrive he organized the First South Carolina Volunteers, a regiment of Negro soldiers. Organized it without authority from the War Department, without proper arms and equipment and without pay for its men.

"He's the man I want to meet," Robert decided. "I'll go see him in the morning."

There was nothing at all to show the Negro could do without a white leader; but there came the Planter which Robert Smalls, the black man, had taken by his own command from the armed state of South Carolina, showing that your race have enterprise, energy, capacity, and may be trusted to go alone, at least on steamboats.

Congressman William Kelley

11. Will the Negro Fight?

It was a strange sensation to walk through free Beaufort. A Union flag floated above the chimneys of the McKees' old home on Prince Street and a sentry guarded the brick path that led to the high front steps. The courtyard of the Arsenal was filled with blue-clad soldiers while across the street Negro children played on the platform of the slave mart.

The Episcopal church was a hospital, the Baptist church a school and the library a shelter for contrabands. Robert paused at the open door of the library, which, as a slave, he had never been permitted to enter. Its shelves were bare, its books having been shipped to the North for sale.

The stores were empty, too. Beaufort's business funneled through the offices of the quartermaster in the red-brick customs house that faced the water. The Army quartermasters were the importers and shippers, the storekeepers and the employers of the contrabands who worked on the wharves.

All of the planters' mansions had been taken over by the military. Robert found General Hunter's headquarters in one of the handsome old houses on Bay Street, overlooking the river. A sentry stopped him at the gate, explaining that the General had gone to Hilton Head for the day.

Disappointed, Robert wandered along the road until he found the camp of the First South Carolinas. He watched the Negro troops in their blue jackets and scarlet pants as they paraded across the fields. When the drill was over, Prince Rivers, who had been a coachman in before-the-war Beaufort, came over to talk to him.

"Working for the gov'ment now." Prince pointed proudly to the sergeant's chevrons on the sleeve of his jacket. "Musket in my hand 'stead of a coachman's whip. Have you seen the free papers Hunter give us?"

Robert looked at the slip of paper that Prince took from his pocket. It was worn from much folding and unfolding.

The bearer, Prince Rivers, a sergeant in the first regiment, South Carolina Volunteers, lately claimed as a slave, having been employed in hostility to the United States, is hereby free forever. His wife and children are also free.

D. Hunter
Major-General Commanding

From the First South camp Robert returned to the waterfront to take the ferry to Lady's Island. Soon he was jogging along the familiar dirt road in an oxcart, with the sun beating down on his head.

The island had never looked so beautiful. It wasn't the roses climbing in wild profusion, or the fields that were white with cotton, or the birds singing in the live oaks. It was the people.

They were dressed differently, in clothes from the Northern contraband boxes, and there was something about the way they held their heads, a new tone in their voices.

"Sweetest music I ever heard was the sound of them guns at Bay Point," Chloe Barnwell told him. "All the masters run and hide, but we stayed here."

The cabins along the Street were freshly white-washed and on Chloe's bare walls were pictures cut from a magazine. She showed him her treasures, a tin wash basin, a mirror, a needle and a tangled skein of thread.

"Lady teachers have a store and we buy there. And that ain't all. Wait'll you see what's in the cotton house."

The rough shed in which cotton had been stored was now a school. "For everyone on Ashdale," Chloe explained. "Children in the daytime; men and women, nights. We's working for the gov'ment now and they's teaching us."

When he drove across the rickety bridge to St. Helena and along the oyster-shell road to the sea, he heard the same thing everywhere. "Gov'ment fighting for me. I'm working for the gov'ment."

There were complaints, of course. Some of the government plantation superintendents were mean, " 'mos'

as mean as old Master." Many were more interested in
the cotton crop than in the corn the Negroes raised
for their food. The pay was low and it came too late.
But there were no whipping trees, no patrols riding
the roads at night. The complaints were those of free
men, who could change jobs when the planting season
was over, who could hope for more pay next year.

Who could hope. It was hope that was changing the
islands, Robert realized, as he returned to Beaufort. It
was hope that put the whitewash on the cabin walls
and cleared the fields of weeds. There was hope in the
eyes of the school children, hope in the faces of the
old people with their whip-scarred backs. It was hope
that made the young men volunteer to fight in "Mr.
Lincoln's army."

Early the next morning Robert presented himself at
General Hunter's headquarters. Hunter was a most un-
military-looking major-general. Sixty years old, with a
dark brown wig and a dyed moustache, he wore a
loose white coat and a straw hat instead of a uniform.
Greeting Robert with a friendly smile, he introduced
him to the officer sitting beside him on the piazza.

"This is Brigadier General Rufus Saxton, in charge
of all abandoned plantations and loyal persons in the
Department of the South. In short, the new military
governor. Rufus, this is Robert Smalls, the man we've
been talking about."

Saxton was a younger man, black-haired, with bushy
whiskers and moustache. He rose from his chair with
his hand outstretched.

"It's an honor to meet you, Mr. Smalls."

Robert took the proffered hand, murmuring his
pleasure at the meeting. What was it Hannah had said
about General Hunter? That he had called her "Mrs."?

This was the first time Robert had ever heard "Mr. Smalls" from the lips of a white man, or had shaken a white man's hand.

Encouraged by their friendliness, Robert told them of his dreams of a Negro army. "Ten thousand colored men in and around the forts of Charleston, ready to strike for their freedom at the first opportunity. Ten thousand blacks, fully armed, would be of more service in South Carolina now than an equal number of white soldiers. They know the country, sir, the swamps and creeks——"

"I hoped to have fifty thousand," Hunter interrupted him. "The Negro regiment has been a marvelous success. The men are sober, attentive and enthusiastic, eager to take the field and be led into action."

"Then why aren't they fighting?" Robert asked. "We could have used them on James Island last month, sir."

Hunter picked up a piece of paper. "I've just written to Secretary Stanton. 'Failing to receive authority to muster the First Regiment of South Carolina Volunteers into the service of the United States, I have disbanded them.'"

"The First South disbanded? But I saw them yesterday."

"Disbanded today," Hunter replied. "I can't go on any longer without pay for the men, proper officers and equipment. I've sent them all home to pick crops. But they're within bugle call of headquarters and can be re-formed and on parade within two hours. Whenever authority for the regiment is given."

Robert still didn't understand. Here was a man who believed in Negro soldiers. Yet he was taking their guns away and sending them back to the fields.

"I've been in Washington recently." General Saxton joined the conversation. "The big question there is, 'Will the Negro fight?' Even Mr. Lincoln says, 'If we were to arm them I fear that in a few weeks the arms would be in the hands of the Rebels.'"

"The President—he said you had no right to free the slaves here." Robert turned to Hunter.

"He said it to the newspapers," Hunter agreed, "but he never sent me any word of disapproval. On the contrary, I believe he rejoiced in my action."

Why would a man say one thing when he thought another? Robert's bewilderment showed in his face.

"He's President of the whole country," General Saxton explained, "and he needs the whole country behind him. The men in the Border states don't want slavery to end. They don't want Negro troops. And I'm afraid there are many in the North who agree with them. There's a song the soldiers sing:

*"To the flag we are pledged, all its foes we abhor,
And we ain't for the Negro, but we are for the war."*

"They are for the war," Hunter repeated. "And they need more soldiers—black soldiers as well as white. That's where you come in."

"Me?"

"You." Hunter thumped the table. "Will the Negro fight? You are the answer to the question."

"Will the Negro fight?" Now it was Saxton's turn. "Every time someone asks that, the answer is 'Look at Smalls and the *Planter*.' Horace Greeley's been running editorials about you every day in the New York *Tribune*."

Robert wriggled uncomfortably in his chair.

"You're going to Washington with a dispatch from me to Secretary Stanton," Saxton announced.

"And messages from me to Stanton and the President," Hunter added. "We expect you to return with official authority to organize a Negro regiment."

Startled, all Robert could think of to say was "Me? Navigate through Washington?"

Both officers laughed. "You're a pilot," Hunter reminded him. "The White House isn't nearly so well fortified as Sumter."

Did he dare to make the trip? Talk to the Secretary of War, the President? The channels of Charleston harbor were one thing, the streets of Washington another.

"You won't go alone," Saxton comforted him. "Reverend Mansfield French, chaplain at the Army hospital here, will accompany you. He's an old anti-slavery man, and a friend of Secretary Chase's."

"Figured you needed a co-pilot," Hunter joked.

It was all arranged. Robert couldn't say "no." He walked home slowly, trying to sort out his thoughts. Not until they were eating supper did he tell Hannah and Lydia the news. Hannah jumped up to throw her arms around him while Elizabeth asked:

"Where's Poppa going?"

"To see the President," Lydia calmly answered. "Stop fussing now and eat your rice."

I was then entrusted by General Hunter with a letter to our country's great War Secretary Stanton. Proceeding to Washington, I was honored with several interviews with President Lincoln and Stanton.

Robert Smalls

12. To See the President

On the sixteenth of August, 1862, Robert Smalls stood on the deck of the steamer *Massachusetts*. Everyone had come from Beaufort to see him off—Hannah, Lydia, Elizabeth and even baby Robert. They had arrived at Hilton Head the day before to do some shopping. At Hannah's insistence, he had taken money from their hoard of greenbacks to buy a new suit, shoes, a hat.

"The Rebels' money, going to meet Mr. Lincoln," she said. "Just think, it might have got to Samuel Kingman's pocket."

Their life in Charleston was so far away that it was hard to remember Samuel Kingman. Nothing had seemed real to Robert in these last few days. The meeting with Reverend French, the last-minute instructions from the two generals, the newspaper reporters at Hilton Head. It was as if he were in a dream and would soon wake up.

The *Massachusetts* tooted her steam whistle and there was a reply from one of the boats rocking at anchor in the bay. A blunt-nosed little steamer, sitting low in the water. It was the *Planter,* awaiting reassignment to the Georgia coast, with the Stars and Stripes floating from her staff. This, at least, was real.

As the *Massachusetts* sailed down Port Royal Bay, the figures on the wharf grew smaller and smaller until they were little more than a blur. When the ship reached the mouth of the harbor, passing Fort Walker and Fort Beauregard, Robert turned from the rail. Nervously, he felt in his breast pocket to make sure that the dispatch General Saxton had written to Secretary Stanton was still there. The General had read it to him:

"I very respectfully but urgently request of you authority to enroll a force not exceeding 5,000 able-bodied men from among the contrabands in this department. The men to be uniformed, armed, and officered by men detailed from the Army. The rebellion would be very greatly weakened by the escape of thousands of slaves with their families from active rebel masters, if they had such additional security against recaptures as these men, judiciously posted, would afford."

"You don't call them soldiers," Hunter had objected. He would have phrased the dispatch more bluntly.

Saxton laughed. "If we can recruit five thousand Negroes, uniform them, arm them, train them, pay them, let Stanton and Lincoln call them 'contrabands' or 'Native Guards' or whatever words they can find to sweeten the pill that the Border states will have to swallow."

94

Reverend French was in his cabin, talking with a group of soldiers on their way to New York for their first furlough. Robert joined them for a few minutes. Then, restless, he returned to the deck. It was strange to be on a ship and have nothing to do.

He visited the pilot-house, the engine room, the crew's quarters. By lunch time they were off the bar at Charleston, whistling a salute to the Union blockading fleet. When the sun sank into the waters of the Atlantic, they were passing the wooded shores of North Carolina. Three days later the *Massachusetts* dropped anchor at Hampton Roads in Virginia, and Smalls and French disembarked to take a boat up the Potomac to Washington.

From the wharf at the foot of Sixth Street they walked toward the center of the city, in search of a boarding house. Robert was disappointed by his first sight of Washington. The Capitol, with its classic columns and broad porticos, stood on a hill overlooking the river. Its original wooden dome had been removed ten years earlier to make way for a larger cast-iron structure. The new dome, still unfinished, was hidden by ropes and scaffolding, while marble columns and workmen's sheds littered the ground.

It was a city where fine buildings and shanties stood side by side. A marble palace housed the Post Office, a Greek temple the Treasury Department, but in nearby alleyways, shabby boarding houses and tumbledown shacks disfigured the landscape. The broad stretches of Pennsylvania Avenue, the city's main thoroughfare, were covered with dust in dry weather and mud when it rained. An elegant cream and white street car ran from the Capitol to the State Department, its horses stepping high to avoid the flocks of geese that roamed the streets. On this hot August day, pigs were wallowing in the dust on Capitol Hill and the smell of garbage from the canal that bordered the President's Park was almost overpowering.

Early the next morning the two men from South Carolina presented themselves at the dingy brick building on Seventeenth Street, where the War Department was at work. For one hour each day, Secretary Stanton stood in the reception room to listen to requests from the public. Politicians, Army officers seeking promotion, manufacturers with uniforms and blankets to sell, inventors with new fangled rifles to demonstrate, crowded the rooms. Each must state his business briefly and publicly.

When it was their turn, Smalls and French shouldered their way to the front of the room where the Secretary stood behind a high writing desk. Stanton was a short-legged figure with steel-rimmed spectacles and a long, graying beard. Acknowledging their introductions with a grunt, he quickly read through Saxton's and Hunter's letters.

Questions followed, abrupt, pointed questions. The number of Negroes in the coastal areas . . . the mood of the contrabands on the islands . . . What made Robert think that the slaves of Charleston would fight for the Union?

For a moment it seemed as if the Secretary were interested, as if he were considering Saxton's request and regretting the disbanding of the First South. Then he folded the letters and handed them to a clerk.

"Mr. Lincoln declines to receive Indians or Negroes as troops," he coldly announced.

Stanton beckoned to his next caller. Was this to be their dismissal? As they turned to leave, he leaned across the desk. In a voice that was hardly more than a whisper he advised, "Go talk to the President. Then come back and see me again."

Outside, walking through the wooden turnstile gate that separated the War Department from the White House grounds, French was jubilant.

"Don't let his gruff manner disturb you," he told Robert. "Remember, he told us to come back."

They crossed the wooded lawn and walked around to the east entrance of the White House. It was a fine building, Robert thought, but no finer than many of the planters' homes in Beaufort and Charleston.

Inside, there were crowds of people. They sat in the parlors, slouched along the corridor walls and stood in a line that stretched up the broad staircase to the door of the President's office.

"Office seekers, businessmen, mothers asking clemency for sons who've deserted, cranks with a sure-fire plan for winning the war by next Thursday. Mr. Lincoln doesn't turn anyone away," French explained.

When he tired of waiting in line, Robert explored the building. The interior was far grander than the outside had led him to expect. In the East Room, where big state receptions were held, a red velvet carpet covered the floor and crimson draperies hung beside lace-curtained windows. The walls were white and gold, and in the far corner of the long room there was a huge, newly gilded piano. He tried to picture the room at night when the crystal chandeliers were lit and the ladies in their ball gowns and gentlemen in their dress coats came to meet the President. He would have to remember it all to tell Hannah and Lydia.

The line moved at a snail's pace. It was not until the afternoon of their second day of waiting that Robert and his companion reached the door of Abraham Lincoln's office. The President was seated behind his desk in a low chair, his legs extended in front of him. Slowly he drew in his feet. Slowly he rose, continuing to rise until he towered above them. It was like the drawing out of a telescope, Robert thought.

Mr. Lincoln extended his hand in welcome. "I've heard of you, Mr. Smalls. Secretary Welles has told me of your achievement."

Offering them seats, he paced back and forth. "Are you seeking office?"

When both men denied this, a faint smile crossed the President's face. "I'm glad to hear that. My chief trouble comes from that class of persons. Then you're going to ask me to emancipate the slaves," he guessed.

Smalls and French shook their heads and the President gave a mock sigh of relief. "All spring and summer I've been besieged by deputations—Quakers, abolitionists, Radical Republicans on one side, and representatives of the Border States on the other. Did you see Mr. Greeley's scolding editorial in the *Tribune* on Tuesday? I'm just writing an answer to it."

Horace Greeley had urged the President to free all slaves belonging to the Rebels. Robert wondered how the President was answering him.

"Well then, perhaps you've come to collect your prize money?"

Mr. Lincoln was trying to put him at ease, but the words were still sticking in Robert's throat. "I plan to visit the Navy Department," he gulped, "but that isn't my mission now."

"We've come to talk about Negro troops," Reverend French spoke up.

The President walked to the window with his head

bowed and his hands clasped behind him. For a long moment he stared out at the Potomac. Then he turned back to Robert.

"What made you take the gunboat?"

Robert could feel the blood rushing to his face. His palms were wet with perspiration as he began to tell the tall man with the sad eyes what it was like to be a slave, to have someone own your wife and child, with power of life and death over them, to be a "boy" when you felt like a man. His awe of the President and his office left him and he found himself talking freely of his efforts to purchase Hannah, his feelings when Sumter fell.

Emboldened by Mr. Lincoln's sympathetic interest, Robert tried to change the subject to the First South and General Hunter. But at each attempt to bring up Negro troops the President sidetracked him with another question about the *Planter* and himself.

Suddenly Mr. Lincoln looked tired. He took off his spectacles and began to polish them. "We've got to be very cautious how we manage the Negro question." It was as if he were thinking aloud.

"If we're not, we shall be like the barber out in Illinois who was shaving a fellow with a hatchet face and lantern jaws like mine. The barber stuck his fingers in his customer's mouth to make his cheek stick out, but while shaving away he cut through the fellow's cheek and cut off his own finger. If we're not very careful, we shall do as the barber did."

His voice was nasal, flat. "To arm the Negroes would turn fifty thousand bayonets from the loyal Border states against us that were for us. We should lose more than we should gain."

The two men rose from their chairs. It was clear

that they were expected to leave. At the door, Reverend French hesitated.

"You'll do the right thing, Mr. President. I'm convinced that you are an instrument in the hands of God for freeing the slaves."

A smile lit up the thin, mournful face. "I want to be convinced of that too, Mr. French. Whenever you're in Washington, I shall be glad to have you come and talk to me about it."

Outside, the August heat was oppressive. Robert coughed as a breeze from the river stirred up the dust on the street.

"Then we've failed?"

"No. Now we go back to Stanton." Reverend French had been on missions to Washington before.

At the War Department, the Secretary beckoned to them as soon as they entered the room.

"You've talked with the President?"

He listened impatiently as they told him of their interview, frowning and tapping his fingers on the desk when Robert repeated Lincoln's story about the barber.

"Come see me again on Monday," he said when they had finished. "Not here. Upstairs in my office at two."

There was not a flicker of expression in the near-sighted eyes, no hint of the Secretary's feelings. He scarcely seemed to be paying attention to what they were saying. Yet he had told them to return!

With fast-beating hearts they climbed the two flights of stairs to Stanton's office on Monday. The *Tribune* had just printed the President's answer to Horace Greeley:

"My paramount object in this struggle is to save the Union, and is not either to save or to destroy slavery.

If I could save the Union without freeing any slave, I would do it; and if I could save it by freeing all the slaves, I would do it; and if I could save it by freeing some and leaving others alone, I would also do that."

It wasn't the kind of answer Robert had hoped to see. In the face of it, what could Stanton tell them?

Promptly at two, the door to the Secretary's office opened and a clerk ushered them inside. Stanton looked up from the pile of papers on his desk to motion them to sit down.

His first words were, "You've read Lincoln's reply to Greeley." It was a statement, not a question, and the two men nodded.

He stared at them thoughtfully, as if he were making up his mind what to say next. "I have here an order for General Saxton."

Adjusting his spectacles, he began to read. The opening sentences authorized the General to enroll contrabands as laborers in the quartermaster's service. Then Robert straightened up in his chair. Was he hearing correctly?

" 'You are also authorized to arm, uniform, equip and receive into the service of the United States such numbers of volunteers of African descent as you may deem expedient, not exceeding 5,000, and may detail officers to instruct them in military drill, discipline and duty and to command them. The persons so received into service and their officers to be entitled to and receive the same pay and rations as are allowed by law to volunteers in the service.' "

Five thousand Negro soldiers! Robert wanted to laugh, to shout, to cheer. But the Secretary was still reading:

" 'You may turn over to the Navy any number of

colored volunteers that may be required for the Naval service.

" 'By recent act of Congress all men and boys received into the service of the United States, who may have been the slaves of rebel masters are, with their wives, mothers and children, declared to be forever free. You and all in your command will so treat and regard them.' "

Stanton tossed the paper across his desk. "There is a boat leaving Hampton Roads on Friday for Hilton Head. I've made arrangements for your passage. You'll deliver this order to General Saxton immediately. But, gentlemen"—his voice was solemn—"this must never see daylight. It's too much in advance of public sentiment."

Rising from their chairs, French and Smalls attempted to thank the Secretary, to tell him how much the order meant to them, and to the four million black men and women in the South. He silenced them with a shake of his head.

"Don't thank me." For the first time a tired smile lit up his face. "I, too, want to save the Union."

Ten weeks later, General Saxton rode out from Beaufort to Old Fort Plantation, three miles away. Old Fort, with its spacious plantation house, its avenues of stately magnolias, its live oak grove along the river, presented a typical Southern scene. It was a typical Southern setting for an occasion so un-Southern that the whole Confederacy would soon be stirred by it.

White tents dotted the fields where cotton once had bloomed. The field hands were there, but instead of a hoe there was a polished musket in each dark hand, a blue cap on each dark head. They were being mustered into the United States Army, the first official Negro regiment to bear arms in defense of their freedom.

"You're free," General Saxton told them. "You have as good a right to freedom as I have, or any living man. God never made a man to be a slave!"

Each man sprang his cap from his head and swung it high in the air. Each man gave three loud cheers for liberty, for General Saxton, and for the First South Carolina Volunteers.

Six days later the regiment saw action in Georgia. They were still wearing the blue in February, 1866, when, as the 33rd U. S. Colored Troops, they were honorably discharged from the service of the United States. By then they had been joined by a mighty host of dark-skinned men—the First Louisiana Native Guards, the First Kansas Colored Regiment, the Connecticut Colored Volunteers, the First Mississippi Volunteers of African Descent, the Fifty-four Massachusetts, and the rest—who had fought bravely for their country from the Gulf of Mexico to the shores of the Potomac.

Numerous applications have been made by intelligent free colored persons to Senator Pomeroy for passage to Central America. Among the number is mentioned the name of Robert Smalls who, it is said, is now in Washington.

National Republican, August 27, 1862

13. A Public Figure

Robert Smalls never joined the First South Carolinas. During his stay in Washington he suddenly found himself a spokesman for his people. It started with the controversy over colonization.

In an effort to find a solution to the slavery question that would please everyone, President Lincoln had proposed that freed Negroes leave the United States and establish a colony of their own in Central America. Most colored men disliked the President's plan, but it had white backers who were working hard for its acceptance. To forward the scheme they announced the names of prominent Negroes who had agreed to emigrate.

Absorbed in his fight for Negro soldiers, Robert paid little attention to the colonization plan until a

Washington newspaper reported that he had applied for passage to Central America.

"Me? Leave South Carolina? Leave the Union?" Indignantly he discussed the report with Reverend French.

His first impulse was to seek out the paper's editor so that he could denounce the plan and the use of his name. But that was not how things were done in Washington, French explained.

"You must write a letter, a polite, calm letter, to the paper."

The thought was appalling. Robert could steer a boat and shoot a gun, but he had never written a letter in his life. He read only with difficulty and when he scrawled his name he spelled "Robert" with two "r"s. It was all very well for Frederick Douglass and people like that to write, but as for him——

When all the reasons against writing had been gone into, he found himself hunched over the boarding-house table, phrasing and rephrasing his thoughts while Reverend French wrote to his dictation:

"In your paper of yesterday, it is stated that an application has been made by me to Senator Pomeroy for a passage to Central America. I wish it understood that I made no such application; but, at the same time, I would express my cordial approval of every kind and wise effort for the liberation and elevation of my oppressed race."

Robert shook his head when he saw it printed in the newspaper. "Doesn't sound a bit like me."

He was to do many things in the next weeks that weren't a bit like him. The colonization controversy put him in touch with black Washington as well as white. Contrabands were crossing the Long Bridge from Virginia to the capital city by the tens of thousands. Every day more of them arrived to crowd into dingy barracks and broken-down tenements in their search for freedom. Nowhere was there more concern for their well-being than among the Negro citizens of the city, the men and women who had been free for generations.

There were men like William Wormley, owner of one of the capital's leading hotels and a friend of the Congressmen who took rooms with him. There were women like Elizabeth Keckley, Mrs. Lincoln's dressmaker and closest intimate. There were ministers, doctors, teachers, hack drivers, hostlers, barbers, who lived in comfortable homes near Capitol Hill and worshipped in the elegant Fifteenth Street Presbyterian Church on Sundays.

As president of Washington's Contraband Relief Association, Mrs. Keckley persuaded Robert to make his first public speech. Embarrassed at his lack of education, he talked haltingly at first, then with increased assurance, telling about Negro soldiers, asking for schools, books, clothing for the contrabands of the South.

Back in Beaufort after delivering Stanton's order to General Saxton, he had a surprise for Hannah.

"We're going to New York."

New York! If he'd said China or Timbuktu, it wouldn't have seemed much farther away.

"But what about the war?" She raised the first of many objections.

"I'm to make some speeches, telling about life in South Carolina. Both General Saxton and Hunter want me to go. And it's only for a month."

"But I can't leave the children," Hannah argued.

"They're coming along." Robert smiled. "And you too, Ma."

Lydia pondered the invitation for a moment, then refused. "I'm too old. But you go, Hannah," she urged. "It's right that you should."

A few days after their arrival in New York there was big news from Washington. The President had issued a proclamation promising freedom to the slaves in the Rebel states by January 1, 1863. One hundred more days and all of the slaves of the Confederacy would be free! At last Abraham Lincoln had decided that the Union could not be saved without the help of the loyal black men of the South.

The President's proclamation stirred Negro and abolitionist circles in the city and the Smalls'—slaves who had freed themselves—were greeted everywhere with special enthusiasm.

At the Church of the Puritans, a white congregation in downtown Manhattan where Robert, according to a newspaper, "spoke with ease and self-possession," they made many friends. The men of the church raised money for Beaufort's contrabands and the ladies promised to sew a regimental flag for the First South Carolinas.

The climax of their New York trip was a public reception at Shiloh Church, arranged for by Reverend Henry Highland Garnet, a leading Negro minister and orator.

"Nearly all the colored men of New York and Brooklyn were present," the New York *Evening Post* reported on the following day. "The spectacle of a great and intelligent gathering of black men and women to do special honor to a recognized hero, who had honored not only himself but his race, was sufficiently sublime.

"The entire audience, as he was recognized, rose and received him with demonstrations of extreme delight. The scene during the five minutes ensuing was the most remarkable perhaps of its kind that ever occurred.

"The period of the reception and its object, with the new light the congregation felt was dawning on their race, combined to intensify the welcome and to impart to the enthusiastic outbursts of feeling which were manifested an electrifying effect that can scarcely be conceived."

When the cheering died down Robert was given a gold medal showing the *Planter* leaving Charleston harbor. On the reverse side, the medal was inscribed, "Presented to Robert Smalls by the Colored Citizens of New York, October 2, 1862, as a token of their regard for his heroism, his love of liberty, and his patriotism."

Not all of their time in New York was taken up with public appearances. There were free afternoons to take Elizabeth and baby Robert to Barnum's Museum and the Battery and to a hotel on Fifth Avenue where the first passenger elevator had recently been installed. One evening Robert and Hannah saw Edwin Booth play in *Hamlet;* on another they went to the Academy of Music to hear Carlotta Patti, sister of the famous Adelina, sing.

Of all the city's sights, they were most impressed with the stores. Nothing in Charleston, or even in Washington, could equal the display of goods in Broadway and Fifth Avenue shops.

Robert thought of Chloe Barnwell's bare cabin and

her attempts to fix it up. How she would marvel at the bolts of cloth, the bed ticks and comforters, the shiny skillets and fragrant soaps.

"Not like the sutlers' stores at home," Hannah pointed out. "They don't have near as good for twice the price."

In the wake of the Army sutlers had set up shops in Hilton Head, where they sold cheap knives and watches, gaudy bandannas and shoddy cloth for many times their value. Soldiers with back pay in their pockets, contrabands with their very first earnings to spend, flocked to the stores, buying whatever was offered them.

"No use telling them they're being cheated," Robert sighed. "They can't get no better."

Out of this conversation came a plan for a store in Beaufort. Robert talked it over with General Saxton when he returned home.

"The people on the islands, they have to learn how to keep house," he explained. "Learn how to buy the things they need for decent living. It's a kind of schooling too, just as important as ABCs."

With Saxton's help the Smalls' opened a store on Bay Street where contrabands could find good merchandise for a fair price. Robert had no intention, however, of clerking behind a counter by day and struggling with columns of figures at night. The war was still going on and he wanted to fight. The only question was, where?

The *Planter* had been transferred from the Navy to the Army. A week after his return from New York, Robert had piloted her up the Broad River to Pocotaligo, leading a fleet of gunboats and transports to destroy the railroad bridges on the Charleston-Savannah line. Soldiers from the *Planter* attacked a Rebel troop train and burned the trestle bridge that spanned the river. Then Rebel cavalry counterattacked, forcing the Yankees to retreat to the shore.

For several hours the *Planter* was under heavy enemy fire. The gunboats assigned to cover her had run aground and she had only her own guns to protect her. Shot and shells struck the pilot-house and bounced from the deck, wounding the commanding officer, before the last soldier was able to climb aboard and Robert could begin the trip downriver.

There was action enough at Pocotaligo but it was the only engagement Robert took part in for many months. Other pilots were ferrying troops to Georgia and Florida, destroying Rebel works and returning with boatloads of contrabands. Other pilots were steaming up the rivers to bring the news of the President's proclamation to the cotton fields and the marsh lands where rice was grown.

But whenever Robert approached Captain Elwell, the Army quartermaster, for an assignment, the captain smiled mysteriously. There were plans afoot, hush-hush plans. His services would be needed soon. Meanwhile he must wait patiently and work in his store.

If there was one thing Robert couldn't do it was to wait patiently. From Elwell's headquarters, he walked to General Saxton's, determined to join the First South Carolina Volunteers. Here too he met mysterious smiles.

"General, I'm going to stop keeping store. I'm going to enlist."

"What?" the General teased. "Enlist when you can make fifty dollars a week keeping store?"

"Yes, sir," Robert insisted. "How can I expect to keep my freedom if I'm not willing to fight for it?

Suppose the Secesh should get back here again? What good would my fifty dollars do me then? Yes, sir, I should enlist if I were making a thousand dollars a week."

It was no use. The General would not accept his enlistment. Not even when the Secesh did return to Beaufort.

It happened on a moonlight night in November, soon after the Pocotaligo expedition. Laborers were still at work along the waterfront, unloading a ship that had arrived that afternoon, when a group of men, four white and one colored, appeared on the wharf.

"We're looking for Robert Smalls. The pilot. Know where he lives?"

A workman paused, considering. "Think he lives on Carteret Street."

"That's right," another agreed. "Corner house, Carteret and Bay."

"Carteret Street? Bay?" The stranger questioned. "Where 'bouts is that?"

"Funny thing," one of the workmen commented when they'd gone. "Those men were civilians. Must be from the North. But they talked like South."

"Talked like South and didn't even know Bay Street. Funny thing," another agreed.

A third laborer abruptly put down the barrel he was carrying. "Didn't talk like just any old South either. They talked like *Charleston*. And they's no white men from Charleston in Beaufort now. Something's wrong."

The crew of men ran from the wharf, up Bay Street to the sentry box, down Bay Street to Carteret. Whistles blew, bugles sounded and a regiment of

112

sleepy soldiers tumbled from their cots to answer the alarm.

Awakened by the commotion, Robert looked out of the window. The yard was swarming with soldiers. A young lieutenant, trying to maintain his military bearing as he tucked his nightshirt into his trousers, was questioning some men in civilian dress.

Robert threw on his jacket and ran downstairs.

"Smalls?" the lieutenant asked. "Know these men?"

It was hard to make out the faces in the moonlight until someone held up a lantern. Three of the men were strangers to Robert but two he knew. The colored man and one of the white men had worked with him in Simmons' yard.

"Thomas—Gabe—what are you doing here?"

Both men hung their heads. It was the lieutenant who answered for them.

"There's a reward for you. Four thousand dollars for your capture. They crossed our lines at Port Royal Ferry planning to kidnap you and bring you back to Charleston."

Robert drew a deep breath. "You tell your masters I'll return to Charleston under my own power. When I can guide a Union fleet up to the docks of the city."

There was little sleep for the Smalls family that night, or for anyone else in Beaufort. Fearful that the captured men were only an advance party, a company of soldiers remained in the yard while others patrolled the nearby streets. At dawn, Hannah rose to make coffee for their guards and Robert started off on another trip to Elwell's office.

The trip was wasted. Not until the short Carolina winter had ended and daffodils were blooming in Beaufort gardens did the quartermaster send for him.

"I'm putting you on the Army payroll starting the first of March. Pilot, at fifty dollars a month."

Robert smiled his thanks. "On the *Planter?*"

Elwell shook his head. "You're going to be working for the Navy. Report to Du Pont on Monday next."

The morning sun was shining on the waters of Port Royal Bay on Monday when Robert climbed the ship's ladder to the deck of the *Wabash*. Du Pont, now a rear admiral, was in his cabin with Captain Rhind, the officer with whom Robert had worked on the North Edisto. The two men were studying a map—a map of Charleston harbor.

The Admiral looked up as Robert entered. Without any preliminaries, he announced, "We're going to attack Fort Sumter with a fleet of ironclads. Captain Rhind requests you as his pilot. Will you accept the assignment?"

The ships will open fire on Fort Sumter when within easy range.

Admiral Samuel du Pont, April 6, 1863

14. At the Gates of Charleston

Would he accept the assignment? Robert left the *Wabash* with shining eyes. An ironclad was every sailor's dream of a fighting ship. While he was still in Charleston the *Monitor* had met the Rebel *Merrimac* in an historic naval battle at Hampton Roads. Only a quarter the size of the Rebel ship, the *Monitor* had a metal-plated deck almost level with the water and a revolving steel turret in which her guns were concealed. Everyone laughed at the "cheesebox on a raft," "the tin can on a shingle" until the *Monitor* fought the mighty *Merrimac* to a standstill and signalled the end of wooden fighting ships.

Now there were nine Union ironclads ready to be tested in battle against the forts in Charleston harbor. One by one they sailed from the North to drop anchor in Port Royal Bay: the *Ironsides,* flagship of the fleet; the *Weehawken,* the *Montauk,* the *Passaic* and four others, all ships of monitor design. Last to arrive was the *Keokuk,* a double-turreted monster, smaller than the monitors, with sloping sides and a deck five feet above the water. Her commander was to be Captain Rhind; her pilot, Robert Smalls.

The expedition was timed for early April, when the spring tides brought deeper water to the Charleston bar. Robert had only a few days to familiarize himself with the strange new ship. She was awkward to handle compared to the *Planter* and in cloudy weather he found it difficult to see through the narrow slits of the pilot-house. Nevertheless, he was as pleased with her as a child with a new toy.

On the fifth of April, 1863, Smalls' twenty-fourth birthday, the ironclad fleet assembled at the mouth of the North Edisto River. There was a full moon that night and the sea was as smooth as glass. At dawn on the sixth, the ships headed north to Charleston. By afternoon Robert was piloting the *Koekuk* along the main ship channel, replacing buoys that the Confederates had removed. At flood tide on the morning of the seventh, the mailed fleet slowly made its way into Charleston harbor.

The day was warm and through the sight holes in the *Keokuk*'s iron-walled pilot-house Robert could see the sun shining on Sumter's walls. Yellow butterflies rose from Morris Island swamps and white-bellied sea gulls chattered overhead. In the distance there was the city with its citizens lining the waterfront, crowding the roofs, as they had done during that other battle for Fort Sumter, two years earlier. Only this time the tables were turned and the Union was attacking, while the Rebels defended the fort.

Led by the *Weehawken,* with the *Keokuk* bringing up the rear, the fleet proceeded up the channel. There was an hour's delay as the torpedo raft fitted to the

Weehawken's prow became entangled with her anchor cable. Once more they were slowly under way, past Fort Wagner, past Battery Bee, rounding Morris Island, nearer and nearer to their goal.

Suddenly flames shot out from Fort Sumter. There was an ear-splitting crash as cannonballs struck the iron decks. All of the harbor forts had opened fire at once —three hundred guns hurling tons of metal at the little ships, 160 shots finding their mark in a single minute.

The monitors replied, aiming charge after charge at Sumter's brick walls. But it was difficult to maneuver in the narrow channel, hard to find a good position for an attack. On one side of the fort, the ships were stopped by a stout rope, kept afloat by beer casks, on which the Rebels had hung nets and torpedoes. On the other side, rows of wooden piles rose ten feet above the water to block the way. Any ship passing there would be met by a second row of piles and a third.

The attack which had started out so bravely began to falter. The *Weehawken*'s propeller was fouled in the Rebel nets. The *Ironsides,* unmanageable in the strong tide, veered off her course, getting in the way of the ships which followed her. Soon Admiral du Pont was signalling to disregard the order of battle and it became every ship for herself against the enemy.

In the pilot-house of the *Keokuk,* Captain Rhind shouted in Robert's ear, "Think you can pass the others and bring us up to Sumter?"

Without turning his head, Robert nodded. It was useless to try to talk above the roar of the guns, but he had a plan. The *Keokuk* could navigate in shallower water than the monitors. If he followed the outer edge of the channel he could swing around the jammed-up ships and pull in close to the fort. It was a route he had traveled many times before.

In a matter of minutes, the *Keokuk* passed the monitor fleet and was cruising in the shadow of Sumter's sheer walls, a tiny David against a giant Goliath. Her gunners, stripped to the waist, rapidly loaded the cannon and ran them to the portholes. The portholes were opened, the turrets spun round and the gun muzzles spurted flames as Rhind repeated the command, "Ready, fire! Ready, fire!"

When the wind whipped back the smoke, Robert could see scars on the face of the fort. There was a crater forming in the parapet. If only they could hold their position long enough to breach the wall! But the *Keokuk* was taking far more punishment than her four guns could give. During thirty minutes of concentrated fire from the fort, one hundred shot struck her deck, her hull, her turrets. Below the waterline were holes large enough for a boy to crawl through. Above, the turrets were like sieves, and it wasn't long before the portholes were jammed and the guns useless.

At the height of the battle the wheelsman alongside Robert was struck flush in the face with a shell. Robert was stunned by the explosion, blinded by the man's blood. His hands slipped from the wheel. For a moment the ship drifted lifelessly with the tide. Recovering quickly, Robert staggered forward to grasp the spinning spokes of the wheel. He was scarcely able to see through the dense smoke when he heard the *Ironsides* give the signal to retire.

Slowly the *Keokuk* limped back to the bar, under fire until she was out of Sumter's range. Her flag was in tatters and there were twelve wounded men aboard, including the captain and the quartermaster. Of all the ironclad fleet, she had dared the most and suffered the most.

All through the night the *Keokuk*'s crew was at work pumping out the ship and plugging the holes below her waterline. Just before dawn Robert stretched out on the pilot-house floor for a much-needed rest. He had scarcely closed his eyes when there was a cry from below:

"Man the pumps!"

The rising sun had brought a stiff breeze. The sea was washing in and no amount of pumping could save the ship now. By the time a distress signal was hoisted to the top of her mast, she was settling rapidly. Navy tugs clustered around, removing the wounded, then the rest of the exhausted crew.

There was barely time. Water was pouring into the turrets when Robert jumped overboard and swam to a nearby boat. As he was hauled over the side, the *Keokuk* lurched drunkenly and plunged underneath the waves. Only the tip of her smokestack marked her watery grave.

In the crew's quarters on the *Ironsides,* Robert slept fitfully. Bruised and sore, aching in every bone, he was troubled by dreams. As his hammock swayed with the roll of the ship, he thought he heard sounds in the distance. There was a clank of chains, the whistling of a whip, the scream of a man in pain. A reproachful voice whispered in his ear:

"Twice you've come to Charleston to unlock the gates. Twice you've been turned back. When will we be free?"

He had no answer.

The Planter *is still fired at on her daily trips from Stono to Lighthouse Inlet. Persons stand upon the deck of the vessel smoking, as unconcernedly as an excursion party would do on the 4th of July.*

New York *Tribune,* December 19, 1863

15. Captain Smalls, U.S.A.

Through the spring and summer of 1863, Robert remained within sight of Charleston. After the defeat of the ironclads, the Union admirals and generals drew up a new plan for the capture of the Rebel city. Soldiers landing on Morris Island were to capture Fort Wagner, then turn its guns on Sumter.

It was long slow work and Robert was in the thick of it, piloting troop ships for night landings, working to establish camps, communication centers, supply depots and coaling stations. He was unable to return to Beaufort even when a tear-stained note from Hannah informed him that baby Robert had died of the smallpox and that Elizabeth was slowly recovering from the dread disease.

His little son, born in slavery, would never become a free man in the world after the war. His little son whom he'd scarcely known was gone, dead, buried, and there was no time for mourning. For a while it seemed as if the bottom had dropped out of his world and he went about his duties with dull eyes and tight lips.

When Army headquarters were established at Lighthouse Inlet on the southern shore of Morris Island, he was made chief pilot of the inlet. It was a tortuous and ever-changing channel with only four feet of water on the bar at low tide, and he was one of the few Union men who knew its tributary streams and creeks and could follow them—when the time was ripe—to the open waters of Charleston harbor.

From his boat off shore, he watched the soldiers cross the beach at twilight for their first attack on Fort Wagner. He saw the bursting shells and the bayonets glistening in the moonlight on the parapets. He heard the thunder of the guns, the Rebel yells, and then, as a dark cloud blotted out the moon, the bugles sounding "Retreat."

When the sun rose on the tide-washed beach he helped to bury the dead in the sandhills and move the wounded to the field hospital where Clara Barton and her nurses waited to tend them. For the first time in weeks he forgot his personal sorrow in the face of the death and destruction that surrounded him. There were 1,500 Union casualties on that one summer night, 250 of them Negro soldiers who had led the assault and fought bravely against insuperable odds.

All during the scorching summer, with the sun beating down on the sand and the beach flies and mosquitoes stinging with a special ferocity, the Union men inched their way across the Morris Island beaches. In the soft black mud of the marshes, engineers built platforms of logs on which cannon were mounted.

Shells from the Swamp Angel, the soldiers' nickname for the heaviest cannon, reached downtown Charleston, five miles away.

Each day, the *Ironsides* led the monitor fleet across the bar to attack from the water. Each night, under powerful calcium lights that had been sent from New York, the Army took over the ceaseless bombardment. At last, after fifty-eight days and nights of steady fire, the Rebels abandoned Fort Wagner and the Union forces moved in.

After the fall of Wagner, Robert was transferred to the *Planter*. It was good to be back, to walk the familiar deck and feel the ship respond when he grasped her wheel. Some nights when it was quiet, he listened to the bells of Charleston and wondered how his friends there were faring. With the city under daily bombardment, many of its inhabitants had fled far inland. Those who were left, black as well as white, were working on the harbor defenses.

The Rebels were not giving up easily. The troops they had moved from Wagner were installed in new batteries on the islands near the city and resistance was almost as strong as ever. Union cannon had reduced Fort Sumter to a shapeless pile of bricks. Its guns were buried under mountains of dust and concrete, but its garrison refused to surrender.

Aboard the *Planter,* Robert made daily trips up the inlets and along the creeks, ferrying soldiers to new outposts and bringing in their supplies and mail. After the long summer at Lighthouse Inlet he had grown used to the sights and sounds of war. He no longer winced when he heard the cries of men in battle or when, weeks afterward, he stubbed his toe on a grinning skull, half-buried in the sand. He was constantly under fire, and dodging bullets, ducking when an exploding shell sent fragments across the deck seemed a part of everyday life.

The days grew short. The nights grew cool. As Thanksgiving Day approached, General Gillmore, the Union commander, proclaimed a holiday for the Morris Island forces. On the day before Thanksgiving the *Planter* sailed down to the Stono to fetch slaughtered beeves and hogs for the soldiers' feast.

The ship was returning through Folly Island Creek when Rebel batteries at Secessionville opened fire. The creek was narrow and the batteries, on a high bluff overlooking the water, found the *Planter* an easy mark. At the wheel, Robert wondered why the gun crew was not answering the attack. Suddenly the door of the pilot-house was thrown open.

Captain Nickerson, an officer from Cape Cod who was new to the Department of the South, stood in the doorway. "Beach the boat, Rob, before they kill us all," he shouted. "We'll surrender."

"Nothing to worry about, sir." Robert tried to soothe him. "We'll soon be out of their range."

The captain would not be soothed. Pale and distraught, he repeated the order to surrender.

Robert was angry. Surrender the *Planter*? Turn over *his* ship to the Rebels, who would shoot down every Negro crewman in cold blood? Pushing past the panic-stricken captain, he took command.

It wasn't long before the *Planter*'s guns were answering the Rebel fire. Enemy shells struck the smokestack, the lookout tower, the roof of the pilot-house, but the ship forged full steam ahead. While the captain hid in the coal bunker, Robert stayed at the wheel, shouting orders to the crew.

Not until the *Planter* rounded the bend into Lighthouse Inlet did he turn over his post to one of the sailors. Powder from the shell that struck the pilothouse had burned his eyes, almost blinding him. For the rest of his life he would wear glasses as a souvenir of this engagement.

The injury to his eyes, painful though it was, was the least of his worries at the moment. What would happen when Captain Nickerson crawled from the coal bunker? Would he denounce him for disobeying orders, ask for his discharge from the Army?

Smalls was grim and silent when the ship tied up at the dock, but when he left the field hospital the following day there was a broad smile on his face. In the pocket of his pea jacket was a copy of an order from J. J. Elwell, who was now a lieutenant colonel.

"You will please place Robert Smalls in charge of the United States transport *Planter*, as captain," Elwell had written. "He is an excellent pilot, of undoubted bravery, and in every respect worthy of the position. This is due him as a proper recognition of his heroism and services. The present captain is a coward, though a white man. Dismiss him, therefore, and give the steamer to this brave black Saxon."

All along the beach, soldiers were celebrating Thanksgiving. Captain Smalls joined them, watching wheelbarrow and sack races and cheering the man who climbed a greased pole twenty feet high to win a pair of trousers with a month's pay in the pocket.

He had much to be thankful for. His pay as captain would be $150 a month, enough to support his family in unaccustomed luxury, to feed, clothe, and educate them well.

He had much to be thankful for. A week after the

holiday when the *Planter* picked up the soldiers' mail he learned from a New York newspaper that "Mrs. Robert Smalls has just been delivered of a baby girl." Soon afterwards there was a message from Hannah confirming the good news.

"We've named her Sarah," Hannah wrote, "and she looks just like you."

The year that had started so badly with the sinking of the *Keokuk* and baby Robert's death was ending well.

"What are those coming?" asked the Yankee soldier.
"Negro soldiers," said his companion.
"Damn 'em!"
"What have they got with 'em?"
"Why, some Secesh prisoners."
"Bully for the Negroes."

The Atlantic Monthly, September, 1863

16. Storming the Fortress

Robert spent the Christmas holidays in Beaufort, his first shore leave for many months. Elizabeth leaped into his arms when he opened the door.

"Poppa, Poppa," she shouted, "I go to school now and we have a new baby and I'm going to be in a parade."

He swung her around, laughing. "You've grown a foot, Liz. I can't hardly pick you up any more."

"I'm the fifth biggest girl in my class and I read the best," she informed him.

"Who says so?" he teased.

"Miss Forten. She's my teacher so she ought to know. She knows everything."

As he listened to Elizabeth's chatter, Robert managed to greet Hannah and his mother and peek at the new baby. She was tiny, all eyes and nose. It was hard to remember that Elizabeth had ever been so small. A shadow crossed his face as he thought of Robert, and he reached for Hannah's hand.

"How do you like our Union baby?" she smiled.

"She's fine. Everything's fine. Lord, it's good to be home again."

They sat up late talking, bringing each other up to date on the news. In the months he'd been away there were many changes in Beaufort. The ex-slaves were no longer "contrabands." The word was "freedmen" now.

"And what's more," Lydia said, "freedmen are buying land, raising their own cotton and corn. Government's been dividing up the abandoned plantations and selling them for unpaid taxes."

"There are seventy-five schools in the Department," Hannah added, "and talk of a freedmen's bank. And Liz really can read. Miss Forten says that in a few years we should send her up North to school."

"This Miss Forten-who-knows-everything," Robert joked. "Who is she?"

"Charlotte Forten, from Philadelphia. One of the Negro lady teachers. She studied in Massachusetts and she says there's no prejudice against colored there."

"So you're planning to make Lizzie a teacher? We're certainly coming up in the world."

"Yes, *Captain* Smalls." Hannah smiled at him across the table.

Lydia looked up from her sewing. "No call for you two to get all puffed up. It's not just you that's coming up. It's all of us. Remember last New Year's how General Saxton gave a big celebration for the Emancipation Proclamation? This year the freedmen themselves are arranging the celebration. Committee's been working on it for weeks. Jacob Robinson—he used to belong to the Barnwells—is grand marshal and Prince Rivers is helping him."

Robert knew about the celebration. He had been asked to lead the pilots and engineers in the parade. Early on the morning of January 1st—the first anniversary of the Emancipation Proclamation—he took his place at the front of the line of marchers. Behind him were more than a thousand people: soldiers and sailors, laborers and superintendents of labor, ministers and government officials, teachers and school children.

The skies were overcast but he scarcely felt the piercing south wind as he marched through Beaufort. At the Arsenal the cannon boomed a salute. In front of the slave mart the bands played and the marchers sang, sang so that the whole world could hear:

"*Father Abraham has spoken, and the message has
    been sent;
The prison doors he opened and out the prisoners
    went
To join the sable army of the 'African descent.'*

"*We heard the proclamation, massa hush it as he will.
The bird he sing it to us, hopping on the cotton-
    hill;
And the possum up the gum tree he couldn't keep
    it still.*

"*They said, 'Now, colored brethren, you shall be
    forever free,
From the first of January, eighteen hundred sixty
    three.'
We heard it in the river going rushing to the sea.*

"*So rally, boys, rally, let us never mind the past;*

> *We had a hard road to travel, but our day is*
> *coming fast;*
> *For God is for the right and we have no need to*
> *fear;*
> *The Union must be saved by the colored volunteer."*

Then it was the children's turn. Trudging along Bay Street, they chorused the hymn that the poet Whittier had written especially for them. Robert thought he could make out Elizabeth's high sweet treble as they sang:

> *"The very oaks are greener clad,*
> *The waters brighter smile,*
> *Oh, never shone a day so glad*
> *In sweet St. Helen's Isle.*

> *"For none in all the world before*
> *Were ever glad as we.*
> *We're free on Carolina's shore;*
> *We're all at home and free!"*

Outside of Beaufort, the parade ended at Camp Shaw, the new camp of the First South. From a platform decorated with pictures of John Brown, Toussaint L'Ouverture and Abraham Lincoln, Colonel Elwell and General Saxton greeted the marchers. There was a roar from the crowd as a Negro minister presented a sword to the General "as a testimonial of the gratitude of the freedmen of the South for his sacrifices and labors to secure their liberty, protection and elevation."

Then a second sword appeared, the gift of the freedmen to Colonel Higginson, commander of the First South. Higginson accepted the sword in the name of his regiment.

"It is you who should be honored today," he addressed his men. "You have conducted an enterprise of greater danger than the storming of Fort Wagner. You have stormed the fortress of prejudice against the black man—and won."

After the people had cheered until they could cheer no more, they scrambled to the tables in the rear of the camp and proceeded to eat until they could eat no more.

"Eight roasted oxen and two thousand loaves of bread," Elizabeth proudly announced to her father.

Robert pondered over the celebration when he was back on the *Planter*. "The fortress of prejudice" reminded him of Fort Sumter. Sumter's walls were battered, Sumter's guns were silenced, but the fort was still in Rebel hands.

It was true, as Colonel Higginson said, that the black soldiers had stormed the fortress of prejudice. But had they really conquered it? Was it not still standing, just as Sumter stood in Charleston harbor?

He thought of General Seymour. Last year he and the General had crossed Port Royal Bay together on their way to the *Wabash*. When their boat pulled alongside the flagship, Seymour hailed the officer of the day.

"This boy wants to see the Admiral. Will you please let him know that the boy is waiting?"

"This boy" was Robert, who felt a tight knot of rage gather in his stomach.

Then it came again. "Here, boy. You can go aboard and the officer will tell you when the Admiral is ready to see you."

Robert wanted to reply, to shout in anger, but no words came. He might even have forgotten the incident

—there were others like it—if Charles Nordhoff, a newspaperman, had not been in a nearby boat, noting it down.

"Now Smalls is not a boy," Nordhoff had written. "He is a man and wears a beard sufficient to show it. I blushed for General Seymour when I heard him use the old cant of the slavemaster. Because this gallant fellow happened to have a black skin, he speaks to him in a way that seemed to me contemptibly mean. Smalls seems a very quiet man without the slightest swagger. How he looked or felt when he was called 'boy' in this way I cannot tell you—for I dared not look in the poor fellow's face."

By the time Nordhoff's article was printed in Northern papers and in his book, *The Freedmen of South Carolina*, it was hard to tell who was the "poor fellow," Smalls or Seymour. Even now the story was coming back to plague the General. He had just met defeat in a battle in Florida and the New York *Evening Post* blamed the disaster on his "virulent pro-slavery attitude" as shown by "his contemptuous treatment of Robert Smalls."

This was unfair. Seymour hadn't lost the battle because he'd said "boy" to Robert Smalls and Robert was quick to spring to his defense. With the help of his first mate, he wrote a letter to the *Evening Post* which the embarrassed General forwarded to the newspaper, along with a communication of his own.

The Seymour story had a happy ending, but there were other men in the Department of the South who worked for his dismissal at every opportunity. These were the men Robert was musing about when Sam Brady, his first mate, knocked on his cabin door.

"Wish you'd take a look at the engine, Rob," he said. "We'd best put into Hilton Head for repairs."

"Hilton Head? We're going further than that," Robert smiled. "How'd you like to see Philadelphia?"

"You're fooling?"

"No. The *Planter* needs a major overhaul, new boilers, smokestack, everything. Notice that place on deck where the seams are sprung?"

"Meant to point it out to you." Sam nodded. "The pressure gauge's not right either. But——"

"The drydock at Hilton Head can't handle repairs like we need," Robert continued. "We're going to sail her up to the Navy Yard in Philadelphia."

"But we can't," Sam protested. "The *Planter* was never more than a coastwise steamer. And in the shape she's in now—besides, you don't—from what I hear——" He broke off lamely.

Robert swiveled around in his chair. "Sit down, Sam. What do you hear?" His tone was cold, formal.

"Oh, you know how men talk." Sam looked uncomfortable. "Nothing, really."

The cabin grew quiet, so quiet that they could hear the ticking of Captain Relyea's clock on the wall.

"You mean I don't really know anything about running a ship, that I can't read a chart, that, in fact, I can't read?"

Sam flushed. *"I* don't say that, sir. Nor any of the men on the *Planter*. But on some of the other ships— the officers don't like having a Negro as captain, ranking them. You see, Rob"—he talked earnestly now, forgetting his embarrassment—"this Philadelphia trip's a trap. Some of the—men who don't like you, they suggested it to Elwell. Their hope is to run you out of the service, or scare you out. And it is true that you're not familiar with the waters north of Charleston."

"I can learn." Robert's voice dared anyone to deny it.

"Course you can. But there's the *Planter*, too. Suppose we hit a storm off Cape Hatteras? She'll be pounded to bits."

"Hurricane season's months away. Won't be any storms when we go," Robert snapped. "Anyway my little girl tells me Columbus crossed the whole Atlantic in a ship much smaller than the *Planter*. Lizzie's teacher says he had a Negro pilot, too." There was a hint of a smile on Robert's face as he said this.

"Then it's settled?" Sam asked. "We're definitely going?"

"I'm going. The *Planter*'s going. You can ask for a transfer to another ship if you want." Robert tried to look as if he didn't care what the mate decided to do.

Sam flushed again. "If you go, I'll go. Only I know they mean it to trap you. Colonel Elwell's been a good friend, but——"

"Colonel Elwell's still a friend," Robert interrupted. "He told me just where the suggestion came from and pointed out the dangers. But don't you see, Sam." He pounded the desk with his fist. "I've got to spring their trap. It's—well—it's storming the fortress of prejudice. And it's the only salvation for the poor old *Planter*. The Colonel and I figured it all out. We'll put in at Hilton Head first for a patch-up job. Do you know Jim Harding?"

"The old Englishman?"

Robert nodded. "He made the New York to Charleston run close to twenty years. In all kinds of ships and all kinds of weather. I remember seeing him on the waterfront when I was a boy. Got more knowledge of the Atlantic coast in his little finger than your Annapolis men have in all their kit bags put together."

"Not my Annapolis men," Sam protested.

"Anyway," Robert finished, "Harding's going to go over his charts with me."

Two weeks later the *Planter* was ready to leave Hilton Head for her trip to the North. On the day of their departure, Robert inspected his ship. Noting the bullet-scarred deck, the damaged smokestack, the patched-up engines, he wondered what Captain Ferguson would say if he could see his trim little cotton boat now.

"You'll make it." Harding came down to the dock to see them off. "Just always remember the *Planter*'s no ocean liner. Hug the shore and take it slow. A little luck with the weather's all you need."

Their luck with the weather held. Day after day the sun shone on calm seas and day after day the *Planter* steamed along the coast, rounding the capes, sailing through the bays, following Harding's charts. Until they passed Cape Hatteras, the dreaded graveyard of ships, Robert never left the pilot-house. But after that it was smooth sailing and in a week they were at Hampton Roads, taking on fuel for the final lap of the trip.

Two nights later they entered Delaware Bay and sailed up the river to Philadelphia. One engine sputtered and died on the Delaware, but in the morning the crew tied up at the Navy Yard wharf and Robert vaulted the rail to report to the quartermaster.

It was the thirteenth of May, 1864, two years to the day since the *Planter* sailed from her berth in Charleston. Once again, the fortress of prejudice had been successfully stormed.

*Robert Smalls, the hero who had run a Rebel vessel
out of Charleston and given it to the Union fleet was
recently put out of a Thirteenth Street car.*
Philadelphia Press, January 13, 1865

17. Philadelphia

It was not until Robert and Sam saw the *Planter*
hauled out of the water that they realized just how
lucky they had been. Engines, boilers, paddle wheels,
pumps, hydrometers all needed replacing or extensive repairs. In a yard on the Jersey shore of the Delaware, workmen caulked her hull, replanked her deck
and repaired her rails while engineers sent to New
York for new machinery. The days stretched into
weeks and the weeks into months—seven months in
all—before the last coat of paint was dry and the
Planter was ready to return to the South.

During his stay in Philadelphia, Robert determined
to put his free time to good use. Hiring two tutors, Mr.
Bassett who taught him by day and Mr. Catom at
night, he learned to read and to write a passable hand.

"I'm twenty-five years old and today I read my first
book. See that you do better," he wrote in a letter to
Elizabeth.

He chuckled over her answer. "Dear Poppa," she'd
written, in a hand as legible as his own, "I'm only six

and a half and I read two books already. See that you catch up to me."

Throughout his life Robert Smalls never caught up with his daughter as far as reading books was concerned. Books were too slow, too long. He was in a hurry to learn what went on in the world and for this he turned to newspapers. While he was in Philadelphia he read the *Press* and *Bulletin,* the New York *Tribune* and *Herald,* the Washington *Republican* and *Star.*

It was the summer of 1864 and he was absorbed in the news of the election campaign. A few days after the *Planter*'s arrival in Philadelphia, there had been a meeting in Beaufort to elect delegates to the National Union Convention in Baltimore. Robert had been chosen as one of the delegates, the first time in United States history that a Negro had been elected to represent his state at a national political convention. Although he was unable to attend the convention he eagerly followed its progress in the newspapers.

The Baltimore convention nominated Abraham Lincoln for President and Andrew Johnson for Vice-President. General George McClellan was running against Lincoln. McClellan favored an immediate peace with the Rebels and opposed the emancipation of the slaves. If he were elected only those slaves who had escaped to the North would be free.

In the summer of 1864 the war was going badly for the Union and politicians everywhere were sure that McClellan would win. Lincoln's only hope for election depended on good news from the battlefields.

At last, early in September, the good news came. Admiral Farragut had captured Mobile, the Rebels' last port on the Gulf of Mexico, and a wire from Gen-

eral Sherman announced, "Atlanta is ours, and fairly won." After that no one wanted to end the war until the Rebels were soundly beaten. On Election Day, twenty-two of the twenty-five Union states cast their ballots for Abraham Lincoln.

Long before the election Robert had been caught up in the busy life of the city. With letters of introduction from Elizabeth's teacher, Miss Forten-who-knows-everything, he had met the leading lights of the old abolitionist movement. Soon he was in demand as a speaker and there were weekly announcements in the newspapers: "Captain Smalls will address the General Conference of the African Methodist Episcopal Church . . . Captain Smalls will speak at the meeting of the Freedmens Relief Association at Concert Hall . . . Captain Smalls will attend a fair given by the ladies of the Sanitary Commission."

At first he spoke for the South, the new South that would come into being when the war was won. Later he became the central figure in a controversy of Philadelphia's own making. It began on a blustery fall day when he and Sam were returning from a visit to the shipyard. It started to rain and Sam suggested that they take a street car back to their rooms. The two men climbed aboard and were fumbling in their pockets for fare when the conductor loomed above them.

Frowning at Robert, he announced, "You must leave your seat and go forward." A jerk of his head indicated the open platform of the car where the rain was beating down.

"I'm accustomed to go forward." Robert spoke pleasantly. "But why?"

"We allow no man of your color in these cars. You must go forward."

Robert made no move to rise. His voice was still quiet as he answered, "I can't obey that order. I'll remain aft."

The conductor turned red with anger. He leaned over, ready to pull Robert to his feet. Still fighting for calm, Robert asked, "Is it the law?"

When the conductor nodded, he stood up. "I won't disobey the law. But I won't ride on the platform either. Stop the car so that I can leave."

To the conductor's dismay, Sam rose too, announcing in tones that every passenger could hear:

"I will follow my captain."

When they were standing on the street corner in the pelting rain, with the need for dignity gone, Robert exploded. Colored men were allowed on street cars in New York, in Washington, and even in New Orleans, but here in the City of Brotherly Love, in the shadow of the Liberty Bell, they must walk. Something must be done about it!

Many things were quickly done. As newspapers across the nation carried the story of the war hero who had been put off a Philadelphia street car, Philadelphians signed an "Appeal to the Boards of Presidents of the City Passenger Railways." Quakers, deciding to boycott the cars until Negro passengers were admitted, joined with abolitionists in organizing a mass meeting at Concert Hall at which men like Jay Cooke, the financier, and Matthias Baldwin, the locomotive builder, were prominent speakers.

Under the storm of protest some of the street railway companies gave in, while others ran special cars labeled "Colored." It was not until 1867, however, that the state legislature passed a law forbidding discrimination and the controversy was finally settled.

Long before that time Robert Smalls was back in South Carolina. Early in December he received word to report to the Navy Yard on Federal Street. From the window of the quartermaster's office he could see the *Planter,* riding at anchor in the Delaware River.

Together, he and Sam explored the ship, marveling at the new smokestack and the shiny new pumps and engines. The boilers had been moved from their housing on deck to the hold and the ship seemed more spacious and more seaworthy than she had ever been. Her repairs had cost forty thousand dollars, a considerable sum even at wartime's high prices.

Proudly, Robert sailed her down the Delaware to the open sea. In spite of the winter weather there was no need to worry about the trip back home. Leaving Philadelphia on December 17th, they reached Hilton Head on the 24th. It was Christmas Eve and Robert disembarked quickly, eager to be in Beaufort for the holiday. He was laden with toys, dresses, coats, shoes for Elizabeth and Sarah, for Hannah and Lydia, and he could hardly wait to hear their "ohs" and "ahs."

There were joyous greetings waiting for him, but in the year 1864 the best Christmas gift of all came from an unshaven, weary Santa Claus in a dusty blue Army uniform. General William T. Sherman had completed his march across Georgia to the shores of the Atlantic, cutting the Confederacy in two. As the *Planter* tied up at Hilton Head, signal lanterns on a hill only twenty-five miles away were spelling out a message:

"Tell President Lincoln that General Sherman makes the American people a Christmas present of the city of Savannah with 150 heavy guns and 25,000 bales of cotton."

The war was drawing to a close.

Ye's long been a-comin',
Ye's long been a-comin',
Ye's long been a-comin',
For to take the land.
Freedmen's song, Charleston, 1865

18.   The Slave's Return

Robert's visit with his family was a brief one. On New Year's Day he was ordered to take the *Planter* to Savannah, where every ship in the Department of the South was at work moving Sherman's army into South Carolina. The *Planter's* new paint became scuffed and soiled as she ferried men and mules and wagonloads of supplies across the Savannah River to Carolina's rice swamps or up the coast to camps near Beaufort. By the end of January, the army was on the march again, headed perhaps for Augusta, perhaps for Columbia, perhaps for Charleston. Only Sherman and General Grant in Virginia knew where.

Meanwhile another army had followed in the wake of Sherman's troops. Tens of thousands of slaves left the plantations, left the windowless cabins and the daily tasks to trudge along the roads behind the marching men in blue. Ragged, hungry, barefoot, with all their earthly goods on their backs and a dream in their hearts, they crowded into Savannah. They were looking for land, for work, for schools. In the cold of January they slept under sheds, in abandoned houses, churches, outdoors along the waterfront. Hundreds died and thousands more arrived to take their places.

Before General Sherman left Savannah he issued a special field order. The Sea Islands from Charleston south, the rice fields along the rivers for thirty miles back from the sea, the country bordering the St. Johns River in Florida were to be divided into forty-acre farms for his freedmen's army. Appointed Inspector of Settlements and Plantations, General Saxton was in charge of the distribution of the land, with the *Planter* assigned to transport the ex-slaves to their new homes.

To Robert, rejoicing in his new assignment, Sherman's order meant the dawn of a new day for the freedman. "As important as the Emancipation Proclamation," he wrote to Hannah and Lydia. "Without land, the slaves can never be free, no matter how many bits of paper say they are."

He had other news for his wife and mother too. Along with the new work had come a promotion. Now he was master of his ship, with sole responsibility for hiring and feeding a crew of twenty-six officers and men. The Quartermasters Corps was to pay him $1,937.50 each month, $1,330 for salaries and the balance for food. It was all set forth in a two-page contract, properly signed and witnessed. A contract between the United States Army and "Robert Smalls, Master of the U. S. Transport Steamer *Planter*."

In its way, the contract was almost as momentous as Sherman's order to the man who three years earlier had been a slave. Robert grinned when he thought of Henry McKee and of John Ferguson, former master of the *Planter.* Now it was Robert Smalls who was master—of his ship and of himself.

The settlement of the freedmen on the plantations proceeded slowly. Much of it must wait until the fighting was over, until Rebel troops no longer camped in the rice fields along the river, until Charleston fell.

Until Charleston fell. For four years Robert had been hoping, praying, fighting for this moment, but when it came he was not there to witness it. On the evening of February 17, 1865, Rebel troops withdrew from the city, setting fire to the cotton warehouses and the bridge across the Ashley River as they left.

The fires were still burning the next morning when Union soldiers from the 21st U. S. Colored Troops landed at Fort Sumter, raising the Stars and Stripes on a staff formed from a boathook and an oar. By afternoon they were in Charleston in full force—the 21st U. S. Colored, many of whom had been slaves in the city, and the 54th Massachusetts, a Northern Negro regiment.

The white people hid indoors behind closed shutters while the black soldiers manned pumps and fire engines to fight the flames that threatened to consume the Rebel city. Only the Negroes, slaves yesterday, free men today, came out to greet them. A colored soldier on a mule led an advancing column through White Point Gardens and up Meeting Street. In his hand he carried a white flag on which he had painted LIBERTY in bold black letters. A woman broke away from the crowd to hug his mule and cry, "Thank God, Thank God."

When Robert brought General Saxton to the city a few days later he was shocked at the desolation and destruction. The harbor was dotted with burned-out hulks, the wharves were fire-blackened. St. Michael's steeple had been struck by a shell and the homes along the Battery were littered with marble and brick, shattered chandeliers and crumpled balustrades.

The old stable on East Bay Street was gone and the cobbled streets he used to cross to go to work were covered with weeds and brambles. In front of the Planters Hotel he leaned down to pick dandelions and strawberry blossoms. The hotel's splintered door stood open; its glassless windows were covered with boards.

Ryan's jail and the slave market on Chalmers Street were still standing, scarcely damaged by the Union bombardment. Robert wandered through the pens, gaping at the treadmill, fingering the chains and manacles in the dungeon rooms. As he watched, a Northern reporter took down the iron letters that spelled MART.

"Shipping 'em to Boston," he explained, "along with the steps of the auction block. They'll be exhibited at a fair to raise money for freedmen."

While Robert was walking through the city, word had gone around that "The *Planter* and Captain Smalls are at the dock." By the time he returned to the Battery to meet General Saxton for the trip back to Hilton Head, a crowd had gathered to greet him. There was a round of handshaking and backslapping as he met old friends whom he hadn't seen since slavery days.

General Saxton was setting a date for a public meeting with the freedmen, so that he could explain the Union's plans to Charleston's black citizens, when Robert caught a glimpse of white faces at the fringes of the crowd. They were familiar faces, and for a panic-stricken moment he felt like running away. Instead, he took Saxton's arm and steered him over to meet Captain Ferguson, John Simmons, and the man who had made the *Planter*'s original boilers and engines.

"They built the *Planter*." Robert smiled. "But I put the polish on it."

When it came time to leave, the men and women on the pier surged forward, swinging their arms and raising their voices to give three loud cheers for Captain Smalls. They remained on the dock for a long time as the *Planter* threaded her way through the channel, past Sumter to the sea.

"Too sweet to think of," said one old man who had known Robert when he was a boy.

It was not only the colored people of Charleston who were moved by the drama of Robert Smalls' return. In the spring of 1865, the whole country had its eyes on Charleston—and Smalls.

Charleston was the birthplace of secession, the slave mart of the South, the home of the fire-eaters, the hotheads, the chivalry. Smalls was the ex-slave, courageous, proud, respected, everything Charleston had said a slave could never be.

A newspaper editor in Maine wrote: "We wonder why someone doesn't write a novel, giving it the title 'The Slave's Return,' and making Captain Robert Smalls the hero. Such a colored hero would throw Uncle Tom quite into the background. Since the fall of Charleston he has returned to it under most favorable circumstances. He returns a free and wealthy man, whose name is destined to live longer in memory than many Southern aristocrats who once belonged to the chivalry."

"Charleston," another writer said, "has lived on the spoils of the plundered bondsmen; now her turn has come for the bondsmen to dwell in the deserted places of the slaveocrats. Robert Smalls, the famous Negro captain of the steamboat *Planter,* is able to give bread to half the bank presidents and brokers of Broad Street."

When Robert brought General Saxton to his meeting with Charleston's freedmen, they were met by a grand victory celebration. Ten thousand freedmen had assembled at the Citadel green—marshals on horseback, decorated with red, white and blue rosettes, ministers carrying open Bibles, children singing "John Brown's Body" and, to the same tune, "We'll Hang Jeff Davis to a Sour Apple Tree."

There were tradesmen with banners welcoming General Saxton. The carpenters carried planes; the masons, trowels; the teamsters, whips. The bakers marched with freshly baked crackers strung around their necks. The barbers brought their shears, the blacksmiths their hammers, the wheelwrights their wheels.

In an open carriage drawn by four white horses fifteen women dressed in white represented the slave states. Each of them carried a bouquet of flowers for the General. Behind the carriage was a cart on which an auction block had been mounted. Two men and a child sat on the block while another man played the part of an auctioneer. As the cart traveled along the street he rang a bell and shouted:

"How much am I offered for this good cook? She is an excellent cook, gentlemen. She can make four kinds of mock turtle soup—from beef, fish or fowl.

"Who bids?

"One hundred bid.

"Two hundred bid.

"Who bids?"

The scene was so real that old women in the audience burst into tears, crying, "Give me back my children! Give me back my children!"

Following the auction block were men tied to a long rope, walking as they had walked from Virginia to South Carolina. Then a hearse, with words chalked on its side:

"Slavery's Dead
Who Owns Him?
No One.
Sumter Dug His Grave on the 13th April, 1861."

Women in black marched behind the hearse, followed by firemen carrying signs: "We Know No Master But Ourselves," "Free Homes, Free Schools," "We Can Respect the Purity of a Ballot Box."

The procession stretched on for more than two miles, ending at a metting hall where Reverend French led in the singing of "The Star-Spangled Banner" and the freedmen gave three cheers for Abraham Lincoln and presented flowers to General and Mrs. Saxton. By this time there were tears streaming down Robert's face and he didn't care who noticed them.

It was a day of jubilee and a month of jubilation. Grant was at the gates of Richmond, Sherman in North Carolina and the surrender of General Lee was close at hand. To celebrate the ending of the war, Lincoln and Stanton planned a flag-raising ceremony for Fort Sumter, to take place on April 14, the fourth anniversary of its fall.

On the morning of the great day the *Planter* headed for Sumter with three thousand freedmen aboard. Dressed in their Sunday best, they hung over the gunwales and climbed the rails, crowded almost to suffocation. Hannah, Lydia and the children found shelter in Robert's cabin, along with Major Martin Delany, the Army's first Negro field officer. Robert stood on the roof of the pilot-house, "a prince among them," a

Northern visitor reported, "self-possessed, prompt and proud, giving his orders to the helmsman in ringing tones of command."

The *Planter* dropped anchor alongside the fort where her passengers could watch the distinguished visitors as they arrived from the city. There were Senators and Congressmen, generals and admirals, and such prominent abolitionists as William Lloyd Garrison and Reverend Henry Ward Beecher. Every ship in the harbor was decorated from bowsprit to stern, from foremast to mizzen with flags, banners and bunting.

Inside the fort, Anderson, now a general, carried the battle-stained flag that he had hauled down four years earlier. As the wind blew back his gray hairs, he spoke in a subdued voice.

"After four long, long years of war, I restore to its proper place this flag which floated here during peace. I thank God that I have lived to see this day." With a strong steady pull on the halyard, he lifted the flag to the top of its staff. Bands played and the spectators waved hats and handkerchiefs, hurrah'd and sang, " 'Oh, say can you see.' " From all of the harbor forts, from all of the harbor ships, came the thunder of cannon. For the first and last time the *Planter* fired her guns in Charleston harbor.

When the gun salute was over and the wind had carried away the dark clouds of smoke, Reverend Beecher spoke. "Did I say we brought back the same banner that you bore away, noble and heroic sir?" he addressed himself to Anderson. "It is not the same. When it went down four million people had no flag. Today it rises and four million people cry out, 'Behold our flag!' No more disunion, no more secession, no more slavery!"

148

A day of jubilee and a night of jubilation. In the evening Smalls rowed over to the *Oceanus,* a steamer chartered for the occasion by the members of Reverend Beecher's Brooklyn congregation. One of the Northerners described him as "a stoutly built man, little more than medium height, of intelligent countenance, ready speech, entire self-possession and considerable humor. For more than an hour he submitted to the most rigid catechism, answering every question with surprising intelligence and frequently with genuine wit of repartee."

A night of jubilation and still another day of jubilee. In the morning Zion Church was packed to overflowing as freedmen carried William Lloyd Garrison on their shoulders to the pulpit. There were more speeches, more cheers, more songs and flowers—so many flowers that one of Garrison's companions said, "You began your warfare at the North in the face of rotten eggs and brickbats. Behold, you end it at Charleston on a bed of roses!"

Outside the church, a Brooklyn minister talked to two thousand Negro children. They begged him to invite Abraham Lincoln to visit their new school and he promised to carry their invitation to the President.

At last the jubilation was over. The jubilation was over and all cheers ceased. Returning from Charleston, Robert noticed a steamer with a flag at half mast. "What's the news?" he shouted across the water through his megaphone.

"The President is dead."

The words fell on still air. Robert repeated his question, unwilling to believe that he'd heard correctly. But the answer was the same.

"The President is dead."

You say you have emancipated us. You have; and I thank you for it. But when you turned us loose, you gave us no acres; you turned us loose to the sky, to the storm, to the wrath of our infuriated masters.

Frederick Douglass

19. To Construct Anew

"Lincoln died for we."

The freedmen of the South had lost their friend. All along South Carolina's coast, flags of black cloth floated from the housetops and mourners thronged to funeral services. With trembling hands Hannah stitched black cambric to her dress and pinned scraps of crape on the children's shoulders. Robert walked the streets of Beaufort with a mourning band around his arm.

Everywhere he went troubled people asked him questions. Was it true, now that Lincoln was dead, that the old masters would come back? Was it true that they would take the land away? There were even rumors of the return of slavery.

Robert laughed away the rumors. The President was dead, but there was a new President in the White House and the war was won. Andrew Johnson had accepted the surrender of the last Rebel forces and appointed General Hunter to try Lincoln's assassins in an

Army court. Union soldiers had captured Jefferson Davis and he was now in Hilton Head awaiting shipment to the North.

The news that the onetime President of the Confederacy was aboard the U.S.S. *Clyde* in Port Royal Bay brought crowds to the beaches and filled the harbor boats. Traveling from Beaufort with dispatches from General Saxton, Robert was one of the favored few to board the *Clyde* and see the Davises. He returned home the next day with a small Negro boy and a letter from Mrs. Davis to General Saxton.

"Boy's Jim Limber," he reported to Hannah. "No bigger than Lizzie. Seems he's an orphan Mrs. Davis befriended. She's asking the General to take care of him."

"Please, Poppa"—Elizabeth was listening—"can I go over and play with him? Can I, Poppa?"

"Don't know as you'd want to," Robert chuckled. "He's what they'd call an unreconstructed Rebel. All the way upriver he was fighting me like a tiger and shouting 'Three cheers for President Jeff Davis.'"

Little Jim Limber had a hard time in Beaufort. Loyal to the Davises, who had shown him the only kindness he had ever known, he was tormented by the other children's favorite song, "We'll Hang Jeff Davis to a Sour Apple Tree." More often than not the singing was followed by doubled-up fists and a rain of oyster shells.

"What shall we do with Jim?" General Saxton asked for Robert's advice. "I'm thinking of sending him North to boarding school."

"Guess the North's the best thing," Robert agreed. "I'd take him myself only Lizzie wouldn't have him in the house. Even little Sarah calls him 'Reb.'"

Jim Limber was not the only displaced person in the South the summer after the war. Everywhere in South Carolina people were hungry, homeless, on the move. Crops rotted in the fields as ex-soldiers roamed the war-torn countryside and ex-slaves headed for the coast in search of the land that had been promised them. Local government had collapsed. Confederate money was worthless. The only authority was the Union Army and the newly formed Freedmen's Bureau, which was distributing food and clothing to needy families, white as well as black.

To Robert's delight, General Saxton was appointed state chief of the Bureau. Transferring his headquarters to Charleston, he continued to carry out Sherman's field order. Day after day the *Planter* put out from the wharves with families of ex-slaves. By the end of the summer Robert had moved forty thousand freedmen to the Sea Islands. The fields were green with corn and white with cotton and the freedmen were building homes, schools, churches, and roads. Soon their first peacetime crops—their first free crops —would be ready for harvest.

"But I'm worried, Rob," General Saxton confided in Smalls when he returned from a tour of inspection. "In Washington sympathy's shifted from the ex-slave to the ex-slaveholder. President Johnson's issuing pardons to the Rebels by the dozen and ordering their plantations restored."

"But they can't take back the land," Robert protested. "General Sherman's order gave it to the freedmen. They've cleared it and planted it and built homes there."

They couldn't take back the land, but they did. At first the Freedmen's Bureau defended the freedmen. "The faith of the government is solemnly pledged to maintain them in possession," Saxton said. At first the freedmen defended themselves. Armed with clubs and guns, they refused to allow the planters to set foot on the island beaches.

Then came new orders from Washington. It was the job of the Freedmen's Bureau, the President announced, to restore the land to its former owners. On a windy day in October, Robert set sail for Edisto Island, bringing Major General Howard, head of the Freedmen's Bureau, to a conference with the freedmen.

With mounting anger, he heard Howard ask the Negroes to give up their homes. There were despairing cries of "No, no!" and a man shouted, "Why do you take away our land? You give it to our all-time enemies. That isn't right." A woman rose and began to sing, " 'Nobody knows the trouble I feel. Nobody knows but Jesus.' "

The General was troubled, Robert could see, but he was an Army officer with an order to carry out. He allowed the freedmen to remain on the plantations until their crops were harvested. Then they must leave or hire out to the planters. Only in Beaufort and on the islands nearby were the ex-slaves allowed to hold on to the land they had bought with their wartime earnings.

Less than a year after General Sherman's field order, less than a year after Lincoln's death, the *Planter* was at work carrying freedmen away from the islands. When General Saxton continued to protest against the injustice, he was removed from his post and sent to the North and the *Planter* was turned back to the Army quartermaster.

Robert remained in Charleston for a few more months, ferrying Army officers, government employees and Northern visitors back and forth to Hilton Head. It was discouraging work after the promise of earlier years and he had few regrets when an advertisement was placed in Charleston newspapers:

> CHIEF QUARTERMASTER'S OFFICE,
> DEPARTMENT OF THE CAROLINAS,
> CHARLESTON, S. C., July 30, 1866.
> Will be be sold at Public Auction, at North Commercial Wharf, at 10 o'clock A. M., August 15th, 1866, the U. S. steamer "PLANTER," with all her equipments. The "Planter" is well adapted for carrying cotton, having capacity for one thousand bales. Her hull and machinery are in perfect order. She is 150 feet long; 46 feet beam; 7 feet depth of hold; draught 6 feet; has two tubular boilers; two horizontal high-pressure engines, not connected; diameter of cylinder 20 inches; stroke of piston 6 feet.
> Terms cash, in Government funds.
> C. W. THOMAS,
> Brevet Lieut. Col. and Chief Quartermaster.
> August 1

In the poverty-stricken postwar city no bidders appeared with cash enough to buy the ship. In August, 1866, Robert made his last voyage on the *Planter*, piloting her to Baltimore, where she was sold to a shipping company and his Army contract was stamped ANNULLED.

His first days as a civilian were pure delight. Almost he was able to forget what had happened on the islands, what was happening on the mainland. At a government auction sale the year before, he had purchased the De Treville property on Prince Street, the house that Henry McKee had built thirty years earlier for his bride. For seven hundred dollars he had bought it lock, stock, and barrel, free and clear, even to the slave quarters where he had been born.

A free man now, he walked up the brick path with a springy step, climbing the stairs to hang his old pea jacket on a hook in the wardrobe in the room that had once been Henry McKee's. Mornings he rocked comfortably on the piazza, reading the newspapers and talking to the neighbors. In the afternoons when the sun was warm he wandered through the yard, filling his pockets with the last of the season's pecans and listening to the mocking birds' song.

Sitting at the head of the table in the white-paneled dining room, he marveled at his good fortune. Here was Lydia, wrinkled and gray, but still spry at seventy-six. Here was Hannah, more mature of figure than when he had first met her, but youthful, pretty, wise. In his absence she had become a community leader, treasurer of the Ladies Fair that raised money for needy freedmen.

At the foot of the table were the children. At last he would have time to talk to tiny, bright-eyed Srah, his Union baby. Already she showed signs of musical ability although troubled with an asthmatic cough. Elizabeth was now a sturdy eight-year-old who skipped and shouted and wrestled with the neighborhood boys —when her grandmother wasn't looking.

In addition to their home, he owned a plantation on Lady's Island. This year the caterpillars had gotten most of the crop, but next year it would do better. Tomorrow he was going to talk to Henry Kirby at the livery stable about buying a horse and carriage. The next day he was going to hire a teacher and complete his education.

For three months after his return from the Army he rose with the sun, studying alone from five to seven and with his teacher from seven to nine. During the rest of the day he was in the thick of local affairs. First there was the school, Elizabeth's school.

"Won't be any classes soon, unless something's done about it," she announced at the dinner table one evening.

"Done about what?" her father asked.

"About a building. We're the female sem-in-ary." Elizabeth pronounced the word carefully, having learned it only that day. "They want it back."

Until the war there had never been public schools in South Carolina. The rich educated their children in private seminaries or sent them to the North. The poor, white as well as black, didn't educate their children at all. Now there were nine schools in the Beaufort district, housed in abandoned buildings assigned to them by the Freedmen's Bureau.

All over South Carolina children were singing:

> *"So come, bring your books and slates,*
> *And don't be a fool;*
> *For Uncle Sam is rich enough*
> *To send us all to school."*

"Uncle Sam's not quite rich enough," Mrs. Fogg, the school principal, sighed when Robert went to see her. "The Freedmen's Bureau says we must vacate the seminary in June. The freedmen's aid societies of the North will pay our teachers' salaries, but there's no money for a building."

"Any idea where you'd like the school?" Robert asked.

Mrs. Fogg nodded. "There's a house on Carteret Street, across from the old Beaufort College. It was boarded up all during the war."

"You mean the planters' club, corner Carteret and Washington? Two-story frame house with a good-sized plot?" It was a familiar landmark to Robert, only two streets from his home.

"That's the one," Mrs. Fogg said. "There's room for eight classrooms and a chapel for assemblies and an outbuilding with four more rooms, but——"

"No 'buts.'" Robert reached for his hat. "We're going to get that school."

And get it they did. It took speeches, ladies' fairs, suppers, and exhibitions at which the children recited and sang. Robert collected money from everyone he had ever known in Beaufort and Charleston and made a whirlwind trip to explain the problem to sympathetic audiences in Boston and New York. By spring there was enough money to purchase the old planters' club and deed it forever "To the colored children of Beaufort."

A new coat of brown paint, new desks from the North with tops that lifted up so that books could be stored inside, and the school was ready for its pupils.

"There's just one thing." Mrs. Fogg hesitated. "A bell. We need a bell to call the children to school."

Robert was silent for a moment, trying to remember something that had happened a long time ago. The curfew bell! He hurried over to the jailhouse. Sure enough, the old bronze bell was still there, dismantled, in a shed in the yard. Armed with an order from the Freedmen's Bureau, he had the bell hoisted to the belfry on top of the new school. After dinner that evening he took Elizabeth and Sarah over to see it, telling them of the night the bell tolled, "Get along, Robert. Go home, slave boy."

The colored children of Beaufort had a school and

a bell, but other problems in this new world-after-the-war could not be solved so easily. Night after night, Robert and Hannah sat on their piazza talking with their friends about "reconstruction." Robert had looked up the word in his new dictionary.

"To construct anew, rebuild, make over."

President Johnson had one reconstruction plan, Congress another. Within months of the end of the war, the President had asked the Rebel states to write new state constitutions and elect representatives to Congress.

South Carolina's new constitution contained a series of laws governing the conduct of "persons of color." They were not allowed to follow any occupation except that of farmer or servant without a special license and heavy tax. They could be hanged for stealing a mule, but they couldn't testify against a white man in a law court. "Servants" (black) must rise at dawn, work till sundown. "Masters" (white) could whip them moderately and discharge them at will.

It was not exactly slavery, but it was close enough to it to be frightening to Robert and Hannah. Similar Black Codes were passed by the other Southern states. When the first elections were held Rebel generals, colonels, cabinet officers and even the Vice-President of the Confederacy were chosen as Senators and Congressmen.

"They're the men who fathered secession, who fought the Union. They don't care anything about building anew." The tea cups on the porch table jiggled as Robert slammed down his newspaper. "Restoration's what they want, not reconstruction. First the plantations, then the school buildings—then the slaves."

It wasn't only people like Robert who were angry. In Washington an outraged Congress refused to seat the Southerners when they arrived on Capitol Hill. More was at stake than the laws governing "persons of color." The number of Congressmen from each state depended on the state's population. If four million freedmen—voiceless and voteless—were counted in the states' population, the South would be more powerful in Congress than the North. The men who had started the war, the men who had been traitors, would rule the government they had sought to destroy.

A month before his death Lincoln had written to the Governor of Louisiana: "You are about to have a convention which among other things will probably define the elective franchise. I barely suggest for your private consideration whether some of the colored people may not be let in, as for instance the very intelligent and especially those who have fought gallantly in our ranks. They would probably help in some trying time in the future to keep the jewel of liberty in the family of freedom."

Three years had gone by since Lincoln's letter, three years in which Southern leaders rejected every compromise that Congress offered. "The jewel of liberty" was clearly threatened and there was only one way to defend it—to give the vote to the freedmen. After heated debates, Congress ordered the military governors of the South to register all male citizens "of whatever race, color or previous condition."

Elizabeth ran home from school bursting with the news. "Poppa's got the vote." Soon Sarah took up the chant and the two girls skipped down the street, announcing at every open door and window, "Poppa's got the vote. Poppa's got the vote." By dinner time the house was crowded with excited people and Beaufort's freedmen had formed their first political club.

In the fall of the year, Robert was appointed a registrar of the voters in St. Helena Parish. Men traveled from all over the islands to put down their names "for the gov'ment." When the elections were held a majority voted for a new state constitution, choosing Robert Smalls as one of the men to write it. At last reconstruction was about to begin.

We built school houses, established charitable institutions, built and maintained the penitentiary system, rebuilt the jails and court houses, rebuilt the bridges and re-established the ferries. In short we reconstructed the state and placed it upon the road to prosperity.

Congressman Thomas Miller, Negro,
of South Carolina

20. The Incredible, Hopeful Experiment

"Poppa's got the vote." Elizabeth's chant was still ringing in his ears when Robert arrived in Charleston. He walked along King Street to the Clubhouse, the hall in which the constitutional convention was to meet. Years ago when he had walked this street as a slave boy, in patched pants and hand-me-down shoes, shopkeepers and passers-by had greeted him with smiles. Now that he was a man with his instructions as a delegate in the breast pocket of his new suit he met only silence and unfriendly stares.

"Poppa's got the vote." For three hundred years South Carolina had been ruled by a small group of wealthy landowners. Overnight their world had been turned topsy-turvy—"the maddest, most unscrupulous and infamous revolution in history," a newspaper said

—and the white farmers from the upcountry and the black field hands from the low country were to have an equal voice in running the state.

"Poppa's got the vote." Fingering the bow tie that Hannah had insisted on buying for him, Robert shouldered his way through the crowd at the Clubhouse door. From a seat in the rear of the hall he studied his fellow delegates.

The newspapers called the convention "the Congo," "the circus" and referred to the delegates as "black baboons" and "ring-tailed monkeys." It was true that a majority of the delegates were black men, many of them former slaves. A few were fresh from the plantations, visiting the city for the first time, unable to read and write. Some, however, were men of considerable education who had studied abroad or at colleges in New England. More than half of the white delegates were Southerners. Others Robert recognized as men from the North who had captained regiments of Negro troops or served in the Freedmen's Bureau.

For a few days he sat quietly, struggling to follow parliamentary procedure, listening to the "ring-tailed monkeys" conduct their business. They began modestly, deciding against hiring a chaplain in order to save state funds, voting against unnecessary messengers, clerks and doorkeepers. "Most of us have been used to waiting on ourselves and I think we can do it yet," a delegate pointed out.

How much should they be paid? "I think that three dollars a day is all my services are worth, and further, if I got any more, it would be so much more than I have been in the habit of receiving I might possibly go on a spree and lose the whole of it," one man frankly stated.

Perhaps they felt vengeful against white men? No, for a white man was chosen convention president and the former Governor was invited to give the delegates the benefit of his advice. "We must unite with our white fellow citizens," an ex-slave said. "Can we afford to lose from the councils of state our first men? No, fellow citizens, no! We want only the best and ablest men. And then with a strong pull, and a long pull, and a pull together, up goes South Carolina."

These were the words Robert had been waiting to hear. He forgot the hostile crowds on the street, forgot the sneers in the newspapers, as he pictured what South Carolina could become if everyone pulled together. Decent homes, fair wages, schools. Schools —they were the key that would open the door for the colored children, the club that would knock down the wall between the two races.

From his pocket he took out the sheet of paper that he had been working on in his room each night. Unfolding it, he walked down the aisle to the front of the hall to offer his first motion.

"Whereas, the maintenance of an intelligent government, faithful to the interests and liberties of the people, must in great measure depend upon the intelligence of the people themselves and,

"Whereas, the experience of those states which have opened to the poor and rich alike the opportunities of instruction has demonstrated the utility of common schools in elevating the intellectual character of their population, therefore,

"Resolved, that the Committee on the Constitution be directed to report an article providing for a system of common schools, of different grades, to be open without charge to all classes of persons."

After long hours of debate, his motion was carried. There would be public schools for the first time in the history of the state, with colleges and universities open to all!

For fifty-three days Robert sat in the Clubhouse, attending committee meetings, speaking from the floor, arguing with other delegates, until they had hammered out the most democratic constitution that South Carolina had ever had and one that the state was to live under for many years.

The new document repealed the Black Code, abolished property qualifications for voting, put an end to imprisonment for debt, enlarged the rights of women and gave the state its first divorce law. "Poppa" had the vote and, along with all the other poppas, he had used it wisely.

Even some of the newspapers praised the delegates now. "Beyond all question the best men in the convention are the colored members," the Charleston *Daily News* said. "They have displayed, for the most part, remarkable moderation and dignity." And in the New York *Herald,* "Here in Charleston is being enacted the most incredible, hopeful and yet unbelievable experiment in all the history of mankind."

The convention ended in March, when the palmettoes were putting out tender green shoots and peach and pear trees were blooming in Charleston gardens. Robert thought back to another March, three years earlier, and the jubilee that had ended with Lincoln's death. Perhaps the promise of those days was yet to be fulfilled.

The "incredible, hopeful experiment" continued. Robert was only at home for a few weeks when he was elected to the General Assembly of the state.

Traveling to Columbia, the capital, he was present when the military governor turned over his authority to the newly elected civil governor and South Carolina was formally restored to the Union.

For seven years he spent the winter months in Columbia, at first as a representative, then as a state Senator. He worked hard in the Assembly, fighting for funds for the free schools, speaking for a homestead act and for the establishment of a navy yard at Port Royal. He was a member of numerous committees— Finance, Printing, Mines and Penitentiary—and a regent of the state lunatic asylum.

In the legislature he was one of many lawmakers, some good, some bad, some indifferent. At home, he quickly became a political leader. Elected chairman of the Beaufort County Republican Committee and vice-president of the state Republican organization, he was a delegate to the Republican National Convention which nominated General Ulysses S. Grant for President. In 1871, the Governor appointed him a brigadier general of the state militia, in charge of a regiment of one thousand men. For the rest of his life he was spoken of as "General."

Between sessions of the legislature, Robert spent most of his time in Beaufort and on the islands nearby, talking in the Brick Church on St. Helena, calling a meeting in Beaufort's council chambers to ask for advice on county finances and to receive complaints and suggestions. He spoke bluntly, in the language of the people, praising friends, denouncing enemies.

"My guns are in position and will continue to pour hot shot into the ranks of traitors and adventurers," he would promise.

The weeks before elections were the times that

Elizabeth and Sarah liked best. Then they would be allowed to stay up past their bedtimes to watch the torchlight parades, to see their father riding at the head of his militia company with his horse keeping step to the music of Allen's Brass Band.

When he spoke from the platform in front of Crofut's store, people gave three cheers for General Smalls and sang, to the tune of "The Star-Spangled Banner":

> *"We draw the old wad from the musket today*
> *And into a patriot ballot unroll it;*
> *We stood by the Union in many a fray*
> *And we are, by heaven! the men to control it.*

> *"Brave gentlemen who*
> *Wore the jacket of blue!*
> *Beat time with the ramrods*
> *While I sing to you;*
> *For only the half of our duty is done,*
> *And the ballot must guard what the bullet has won.*

> *"The enemy's ballots may whiten the gale*
> *As they in October are drifting about us;*
> *But we never flinched from the foe's leaden hail*
> *And his paper snow is not likely to rout us."*

After the meetings were over, everyone returned to the house on Prince Street for cakes and tea and talk. Hannah bustled about proudly, making sure that their guests were well-fed. Her Robert had become a man of substance, far beyond their wildest dreams. With their wartime savings invested in houses and lands in Beaufort, they were well-to-do people. She had a cook to assist her with the housework and a coachman to drive their elegant barouche. Next year Elizabeth was going to school in Boston, and they hoped to send Sarah too, as soon as she was old enough.

In Beaufort, everything was peaceful. The new government of South Carolina had decided to strike out boldly, to plan for all manner of public services that had never existed before—schools, orphanages, lunatic asylums, better prisons, aid to the poor and old. A land commissioner had been appointed to buy vacant land and sell it in small parcels to freedmen and poor whites who wanted to farm. A tax program had been drawn up that was fair to all, although it greatly increased the sums that the big planters had to pay.

In Beaufort, where most of the white men were Northerners who had bought land from the government after the battle of Port Royal, everyone was pulling together. But Beaufort was only one small part of the state. In other places, the big planters did everything they could to obstruct the new government. When a Negro entered the University of South Carolina, the teachers resigned and the entire student body left the school. When the land commissioner set out to buy land he was sold worthless swamp land for a high price. The planters met the new tax law by refusing to pay taxes.

"And that's not all." Night after night Robert stormed at the supper table about the latest outrages of the Ku-Klux Klan.

The Klan was a secret society founded by a former Confederate general. Disguised in white gowns and hoods, its members visited Negro and white homes at night. Armed with guns and bullwhips they "persuaded" Republicans to stay away from the polls.

"Look at this announcement." Robert's voice rose higher and higher as he read:

" 'Anthony Thurston, the Negro preacher who was so severely whipped by a party of disguised men lately, asks that we announce to his white friends that from this time forward he will prove himself a better man, will never again make a political speech, deliver a sermon, or vote the Republican ticket.' "

Night after night he read the newspaper reports: "Five Colored Men Shot," "A Funeral Fired Into," "Man Tied Up By Thumbs." Hundreds of people were murdered, including teachers who taught colored children and ministers who preached of the brotherhood of man.

In many counties of South Carolina, U.S. troops and state militia guarded the polls in order to have fair elections or any election at all. The whippings and murders continued until President Grant declared that "a condition of lawlessness and terror" existed and sent federal officers to arrest the Klansmen.

Under the watchful eyes of U.S. soldiers the Klan disappeared. But the former rulers of the state were still not willing to pull together. In place of the Klan they formed taxpayers' groups and charged the new government with extravagance and corruption.

"Of course we're spending money," Robert told the people of his district. "We're not ashamed of the fact that our appropriation for schools is four times greater than before the war. Now in every hamlet and village, the schoolmaster is abroad. Of course our printing bills are high. Is it a cause for boastfulness that the people were kept in ignorance and no public information disseminated among them? We think not."

However, there was just enough truth in the planters' charges to make Robert feel uneasy. When he first went to Columbia, the Assembly met in a public hall. Two years later the State House, damaged during the war, had been rebuilt and handsomely furnished, with carpets on the floors and new gas fixtures to light the evening sessions. The newspapers complained bitterly because the "gibbering, louse-eaten, devil-worshipping barbarians from the jungles of Dahomey, and peripatetic buccaneers from Cape Cod, Memphremagog, Hell and Boston" had voted themselves new chairs and rugs.

The legislators also voted themselves salary increases and some of them accepted bribes from the contractors and railroad men who swarmed down from the North. All over the country it was a time of easy money and corruption. In New York, the Tweed Ring controlled the state. In Washington, the Crédit Mobilier scandal involved Congressmen of high standing and the exposure of the Whisky Ring reached even to the White House. In this atmosphere it was not surprising that some of South Carolina's lawmakers sold their votes.

As the exaggerated reports of extravagance and corruption traveled to the North, Robert received a scolding, fatherly letter from General Saxton.

"When you brought the *Planter* out from Charleston," the General wrote, "you knew where lay the torpedo on the right and the shoals and rocks on the left. You held your helm and soon the *Planter* was safe and you were free.

"The Ship of State of South Carolina is now in stormy waters. The rocks and shoals, torpedoes and hostile guns are ignorance, immorality, dishonesty and corruption in high places. The beacon lights ahead are honesty, intelligence, the schoolhouse and the church. Keep her helm steady toward these and soon the ship shall glide gently by the breakers into the peaceful waters of freedom."

"What Saxton says is true." Robert used the occasion of Emancipation Day to read the letter to the people of Beaufort County. Following a parade of militia men, he dismounted from his horse and climbed to the speaker's stand. Solemnly he read Saxton's letter. Solemnly he pledged to fight for reforms in the reconstruction government.

"The reputation that I gained in bringing out the *Planter* I do not intend to sully by my actions as a member of the state legislature. As well as I knew the beacon lights in the time of the *Planter*, I know the beacon lights now."

Joining with his fellow Republicans in a reform group, he worked for the election of Daniel Chamberlain as Governor of the state. Under Chamberlain, expenses were cut and taxes lowered. There were new streets, new schools, new railroads and factories, and Robert served on a committee to investigate the improper conduct of some members of the legislature.

But it didn't matter how many mistakes were corrected or how many good things accomplished. To the former rulers of South Carolina, reform meant only one thing—a return to 'a white man's government." If they could not accomplish this by fair means it would have to be done by foul.

On a cool fall evening in 1875 the citizens of Beaufort crowded into the Smalls home for a farewell party. Robert had been elected to Congress and in the morning he would take the train to Washington, to represent the people of his district in the capital of the United States.

While his neighbors drank to his health and sang "For He's a Jolly Good Fellow," a different kind of party was being held in Edgefield County, one hundred miles upstate. The hosts in Edgefield were two former Confederate generals, Matthew Butler and Martin Gary. The guests included George Tillman, the man Smalls had defeated in the Congressional race, and his younger brother, Ben. Theirs was a farewell party too, for they were meeting to plot the end of reconstruction.

Swearing a solemn oath "to deliver South Carolina from Negro rule," they chose as their emblem the bloody shirt. All through the winter of 1876, Edgefield ladies stood in their kitchens, dying homespun shirts with Venetian red. All through the winter, the men of Edgefield drilled secret military companies in their barns and cornfields. By spring there were thousands of red-shirted men marching through South Carolina's towns. They had guns and they were ready to use them.

The colored men who took seats in both Senate and House did not appear ignorant or helpless. They were as a rule, studious, earnest and ambitious men.

Congressman James Blaine

21. In Congress

Robert arrived in Washington a few days before the opening of Congress, leaving Hannah in Beaufort to take care of Lydia and Sarah. Washington was a different city from the one he had known during the war. The streets were paved, the Capitol dome finished, and elevators had just been installed in the House and Senate buildings. Ulysses S. Grant was in the White House and on a Capitol stairway hung a painting of Lincoln reading the Emancipation Proclamation to his Cabinet.

On Second Street, not far from the Capitol grounds, he found rooms for rent, two bedrooms and a parlor for entertaining. The second bedroom was for Elizabeth, who was leaving school in Boston to act as his hostess and secretary.

Her train was late, and as he paced the platform at the depot he snapped open his watch to compare it to the big station clock. He felt as if he had been waiting for hours but it was only a few minutes when the stationmaster's whistle sounded and he recognized his daughter's slim figure on the steps of the car.

"Lizzie!" He was startled at the change since he had last seen her. All traces of the tomboy were gone and she was now a young lady, with her curls pinned high on the top of her head and her skirts sweeping the ground.

"Poppa!" Embarrassed by his obvious pleasure in her appearance, she teased him with an answering stare. He had changed too. In his gold-rimmed glasses and his new Prince Albert suit he was no longer the dashing young hero in his pea jacket whom she remembered from the *Planter* days. Now he was a man of the world, substantial, sure of himself—the Honorable Robert Smalls.

Despite his self-assurance, Robert's heart was thumping when he climbed the broad steps of the Capitol the following morning. Elizabeth squeezed his hand as the two parted, she to take a seat in the visitors' gallery and he on the floor of the House.

It was noon on the 6th of December, 1875, when the clerk of the House of Representatives banged his gavel on his desk to announce:

"The hour for the meeting of the 44th Congress of the United States has arrived."

Quickly he called the roll, reading name after name, many of them well known: James Blaine, Joseph Cannon, James Garfield, Samuel Cox, Adlai Stevenson—and Robert Smalls.

Elizabeth felt a glow of pride as she listened to her father take the oath of office.

"I, Robert Smalls, do solemnly swear that I will support and defend the Constitution of the United States against all enemies, foreign and domestic; that I will bear true faith and allegiance to the same and that I will well and faithfully discharge the duties of the office on which I am about to enter. So help me God."

He had traveled a long way from the slave quarters on Prince Street to the Congress of the United States. There was a murmur in the gallery when he rose, whether of approval or disapproval, Elizabeth wasn't sure. Negro Congressmen were no longer a novelty in Washington. Eleven of them had been seated since 1869, including two Senators from Mississippi, and in this Congress there were eight colored men. Nevertheless, the eyes of the country—of the world— were still on them, and they dared not make mistakes.

Back in their rooms after the day's session ended, Robert and Elizabeth sorted through their mail. As a freshman Congressman, he was not expected to take part in debates on national issues. But he had come to the capital intent on representing all of the people in his district and there was much work for him to do.

"Take the land question," he explained to Elizabeth. "The Beaufort homes and plantations that the government sold for nonpayment of taxes. There's still bitter feelings even after all these years."

On one side were the original owners, hoping to recover their forfeited property. On the other were the freedmen, including Robert himself, who had bought the land in good faith and intended to keep it. Only last spring the case of De Treville vs. Smalls had been made the test case in the court in Charleston. Robert, hiring the ablest lawyers he could find, had won the case, securing the freedmen's titles to the land.

"But there's right on the other side too," he continued. "The government collected more money from the sales than the amount of taxes due. That extra money should be paid back, 'stead of sitting in the Treasury like it is now."

Out of the land question came the first bill that the freshman Congressman from South Carolina offered, "A bill for the relief of Henry McKee or his heirs":

"Be it enacted that the Secretary of the Treasury be authorized and directed to pay to Henry McKee or his heirs the amount of the proceeds of the sales of lot D, block 49 and block 130 in the town of Beaufort, Ashdale Plantation situated on Lady's Island and so much of Gray's Hill Plantation as was not reserved for a school farm, less all taxes, costs and legal charges."

Elizabeth frowned as she copied it. Right was right, but her father's consideration for his old master often puzzled her. This was not the first kindness that he had shown to the McKees. Soon after the war, he had looked them up in Charleston, and whenever Mrs. McKee visited in Beaufort he sent his carriage to meet her at the boat landing and take her wherever she wished to go.

Last year she and her children had even visited the Smalls'. Elizabeth was away at school but Sarah had written to tell her about it. "She's a very old lady and the children are old too, almost as old as Poppa," the eleven-year-old had reported.

"She goes around sniffing at a bottle of smelling salts and sometimes she cries. The worst is at meal times. Grandma says she wouldn't like eating with us so she sits at a separate table and everyone has to bring her things. Poppa says we must be nice to her because she was nice to Grandma and him. Mama

176

doesn't say anything, but I think she thinks it's silly, the way I do."

In spite of what Hannah may have thought, Robert continued to be nice to Mrs. McKee. After her husband died, he offered her a house that he owned on the outskirts of Beaufort and in Washington he tried to find work for her children.

Among the newspaper clippings that Elizabeth pasted in a scrapbook there was one from a Georgia newspaper. "While Smalls has gone astray politically," the paper reported, "he has a better heart than all the white scalawags and carpetbaggers put together. He has obtained from the Secretary of the Treasury a promise that the daughter of his old mistress, who is in very destitute circumstances, shall have a clerkship as soon as a vacancy occurs. He also intends nominating the brother of the young lady to a naval cadetship."

The McKee family were not the only South Carolinians who needed government jobs or hoped for appointments to Annapolis and West Point. Mail from home was heavy and Elizabeth's desk was piled high with requests for help. Many evenings she sat up long past midnight, writing letters as her father dictated them. In that first winter in Washington, it was only on special occasions—Elizabeth's eighteenth birthday and Robert's thirty-seventh—that the two took time off for a dinner at Wormley's Hotel or an evening at the theater.

In Congress, Smalls argued for a federal navy yard at Port Royal, for a new customs house and post office in Beaufort, for an improved postal route in Edgefield. Ever since the war, federal troops had occupied the Citadel, Charleston's military college.

Now Robert asked that the government return the building to the city or pay a fair rent for its use. None of his bills were of world-shaking importance. They were only the routine work of a Congressman trying to represent the people of his district.

The long winter passed and the two South Carolinians were beginning to think of Beaufort's early spring when Robert came home one day with a stricken look on his face. He sank into a chair and Elizabeth ran to comfort him.

"Grandma? Mama?" she asked.

Shaking his head, he took a crumpled newspaper from his pocket to read aloud: "The steamer *Planter* was lost off Cape Romain while attempting to assist a stranded vessel."

Elizabeth sighed with relief, but her father was not easily consoled. "I feel as though I'd lost a member of the family," he mourned.

The news of the wreck of the *Planter* was not the only bad news that Robert received that spring. Reports from home were increasingly disturbing. Wade Hampton, a former Confederate general, was running for Governor on the Democratic ticket, opposing Governor Chamberlain. Hampton called himself a moderate, but his backers, the men of Edgefield, frankly announced that they would stop at nothing in order to win the election.

All over the state red-shirted, trigger-happy men were whooping along the roads, giving the old Rebel yell. Their purpose was to frighten people. "Force without violence," Hampton said.

It wasn't long before there was violence, too. In the little town of Hamburg, only thirteen miles from the Tillman homestead, forty members of a Negro militia company were attacked by two thousand white men, attacked with repeating rifles, revolvers and cannon. Men were murdered, buildings burned, homes and stores looted, and the colored citizens of the town fled for their lives.

"The whole affair was a well and secretly planned scheme," an eyewitness wrote to Robert. "General Butler, who lost a leg while fighting in the ranks of the Rebels, was the instigator and the blood-thirsty leader of the massacre. He boasted that that was only the beginning; that the end should not be until after the elections in November."

What had happened in Hamburg could happen in Charleston, Columbia, Beaufort, unless the whole country was made aware of the danger. Turning the letter over to a Washington newspaper for publication, Robert asked for the floor in the House. Congress was debating a bill to send U.S. troops to the Texas border. Robert proposed that the bill be amended to forbid federal troops to leave South Carolina "so long as the militia of the state peaceably assembled are assaulted, disarmed and taken prisoners and then massacred in cold blood." In support of his amendment he read the letter he had received from Hamburg.

Texas border troubles were quickly forgotten as House Democrats united to defend their friends in the South and to attack the freshman Congressman from South Carolina. There was a demand for the name of the author of the letter.

With flashing eyes and a voice charged with emotion, Robert replied, "I will say to the gentleman if he is desirous that the name shall be given in order to have another Negro killed, he will not get it from me. If I give his name General Butler would at once hunt him down. I, sir, had that letter published in the paper. I am responsible for the name."

Congressman Samuel Cox of New York continued the offensive. "The letter has no name attached to it. It is indorsed indeed by the member from South Carolina, but who indorses the gentleman?"

His insulting question went beyond the limits of Congressional courtesy and there were cries of "Oh!" and "Ah!" as Robert promptly answered:

"A majority of thirteen thousand voters."

Cox tried again, reading from a book that attacked South Carolina's reconstruction government. He had read only a few passages when Robert interrupted to ask, "Have you the book there of the City of New York?"

The House rocked with laughter as Cox found himself at a loss for a reply and another New York Congressman pointed out that nothing in South Carolina could match his own state's record of extravagance and dishonesty.

Robert thought he was fighting alone, but as the debate continued his quick wit and ready tongue won him more and more supporters. When Cox thundered, "Give South Carolina a Democratic government and you will see that every man, black and white, will be cared for under the law," it was James Garfield, later to become the country's twentieth President, who shouted in reply:

"As they were at Hamburg!"

When Cox slightingly referred to Smalls as "somebody of a different color and race," Congressman Hoar of Massachusetts jumped up to defend and praise the Negroes in the House.

"They have had to encounter the most formidable

antagonists—the gentleman from New York, perhaps the most trained and experienced debater in this House," Hoar pointed out. "Yet who can cite an instance of an improper utterance in speech or of an undignified or an unbecoming act of a colored Representative?"

Garfield and Hoar were followed by other men, and Smalls' amendment passed by a vote of 86 to 83. Backing up his amendment was a promise from the White House to send additional soldiers to South Carolina if they were needed to keep the peace. By the time Congress adjourned in August there were few newspaper readers in the United States who did not know the story of the Hamburg massacre. Robert had succeeded in alerting the country, but was he not too late?

We stuffed ballot boxes; we shot Negroes; we are not ashamed of it.

Benjamin Tillman of Edgefield

22. 1876

Robert and Elizabeth returned to Beaufort to find South Carolina a vast armed camp. On every public square the clang of muskets could be heard. In every field the note of the bugle or the booming of the fowling piece rang out threateningly. Roads were crowded with bands of mounted men and stores couldn't keep up with the demand for guns or red flannel shirts.

"Every Democrat must feel honor bound to control the vote of at least one Negro," General Butler announced. "Never threaten a man individually. If he deserves to be threatened, the necessities of the times require that he should die."

There were many ways of controlling voters. Employers dismissed Republican workers. Newspapers suggested, "Browbeat and belittle them at all times and in all places." Landlords asked, "Are you going to vote for Hampton?" before they would rent homes, and every white church in the state held special services to pray for a Democratic victory.

To break up Republican meetings the Red Shirts developed a trick known as "Dividing time." Robert first encountered this when, in company with Governor Chamberlain, he traveled up to Edgefield to make a speech.

It was a warm Saturday in August and a crowd was gathering in a picnic grove outside of town. Suddenly, above the music of the band, he could hear horses' hoofs and high-pitched Rebel yells. Before he realized what was happening, an army of red-shirted men were riding through the grove.

Led by General Butler, they dismounted and surrounded the speaker's stand, demanding that half of the meeting time be given to Democratic speakers. The Red Shirts carried pistols and repeating rifles. The audience of men, women, and children was unarmed. There was nothing to do but to agree to their demand.

As the speeches began they pushed in closer and closer, crowding onto the stand and even climbing in the trees close by. When Governor Chamberlain spoke, his words were drowned out by their jeers and catcalls. Then it was Butler's turn.

"Robert Smalls and Daniel Chamberlain have denounced me as a leader of the Ku-Klux," he shouted. "If they don't rise and prove it they stand self-confessed liars."

Robert could hear the clicking of pistols and the heavy breathing of the men in the trees overhead. Before he had a chance to answer Butler's challenge there was a crash and he felt himself falling. Under the weight of the Red Shirts, the stand had collapsed, bringing the meeting to an inglorious end.

Armed men escorted Chamberlain and Smalls to the railroad station, interrupting them whenever they tried to talk with their followers. Even on the train they pursued them with insults and threats—and a solemn warning not to return to Edgefield.

"I'm going back," Robert told Hannah.

"They'll kill you." She was frightened.

"Maybe," he agreed, "but they can't kill us all. Their program's based on fear. Scare the Negro. Discredit the Republican leaders. Then everyone'll vote Democratic. I've got to show that we don't scare easy."

Before he returned to Edgefield there was campaigning to be done at home. Even in Beaufort County some employers were threatening Chamberlain supporters and offering bribes to Negroes if they would join Democratic clubs.

Robert stormed through his district, speaking from the platforms of trains, in Negro schools and churches and at street corner meetings. Often he addressed himself to the women who remembered best what it had been like in slavery days. He made tough, fighting speeches, pulling no punches as he urged people to stand up for their rights despite the pressures that were facing them.

"The ugliest sight I've ever seen is a colored man in a red shirt," he declared.

Late in August his campaign was interrupted by a telegram from the Governor ordering him to proceed immediately to the rice fields along the Combahee River with a company of militia men. The Negro rice workers were on strike and were threatening anyone who worked in the fields.

Instead of calling out the militia, Robert traveled up to Combahee alone, to find himself in the middle of an explosive situation. The sheriff had arrested several strike leaders. On his way to court, strikers had waylaid him and taken his prisoners away. Now he was swearing in a posse of Red Shirts.

Robert was met by a good-natured crowd of men and women, anxious to explain the reasons for the strike. They were being paid in checks instead of money, checks that were good only at the planters' stores. One of the strikers handed Robert a piece of paper.

> .50 Due—Fifty Cents—.50
> to Jonathan Lucas
> or Bearer, for labor under special con-
> tract. Payable on the first January 1880
> J. B. Bissell

As he read it, others began to sing:

> *"We are not afraid to work.*
> *We will labor every day.*
> *All that we want is the greenback.*
> *When the day's work is ended,*
> *Come and bring the pay.*
> *All that we want is the greenback.*
>
> *"Greenbacks forever, come, planters, come.*
> *Up with the greenback and down with the check.*
> *We will labor in your fields*
> *From the morning until night.*
> *All that we want is the greenback.*
>
> *"G. G. Martin, don't you know*
> *That we told you at your store,*
> *All that we want is the greenback?*
> *Henry Fuller, don't delay.*
> *J. B. Bissell, what you say?*
> *All that we want is the greenback."*

Listening to them, Robert had little doubt of the justice of their complaints. But a fight along the Combahee could easily spread to the rest of the state. A fight in which the planters had guns and the strikers only clubs.

"The checks you receive for your labor are an abomination and an outrage," he agreed, "and before I'd work for such worthless stuff I'd see the rice rot on the ground."

On the other hand, "You mustn't interfere with others who desire to work. If any man's willing to work for one cent a day it's nobody's business but his own. A man who tries to prevent his working violates the law and should be punished."

Promising to go bail for them, he convinced the men who had been arrested to give themselves up. Before the sheriff and his posse arrived, the strike leaders accompanied Robert to the courthouse in Beaufort. They were released the following day when the prosecutors were persuaded to withdraw their charges.

Robert wrote to the newspapers and talked with those planters who would listen until some of the workers won their greenbacks and even a raise in pay. But in other places the strike continued and he was once more called upon to act as peacemaker.

Returning to the Combahee early in September, he found the strikers surrounding Bissell's store and threatening a group of planters who were inside. When Robert asked them to leave there were shouted "No's." One man threatened to tie up Robert and give him fifty lashes if he continued to interfere.

For the first time in his life he heard men of his own race say that he had been bought up by white men. Nevertheless, he persisted, afraid not for himself but for the safety of the strikers. If one of the planters were to be injured, no matter how slightly, every Red Shirt in South Carolina would descend on the Combahee district vowing vengeance.

Ignoring their threats, he mounted the steps of the store to face the angry crowd. For hours he argued, pleaded, explained, until their tempers cooled and they agreed to leave.

Hoarse of voice, he returned to Beaufort, staying at home only long enough to pack a bag for a trip to Columbia, where, for five days, he was chairman of the state Republican convention. Compared to the Combahee, Columbia was peaceful. The Republicans formally agreed to back Chamberlain as their candidate for Governor and Smalls for Congress. Rutherford Hayes was endorsed as the Presidential candidate, to run against Samuel Tilden, the Democrats' choice.

On the day the convention ended, shooting broke out in nearby Ellenton. After twenty-five Negroes and two white men had been killed, President Grant decided that "insurrection and domestic violence exist in several counties of the state" and ordered the disbanding of the "rifle clubs who ride up and down by day and night in arms, murdering some peaceable citizens and intimidating others."

The rifle clubs disbanded, only to reorganize under new names: Hampton Musical Club, Mother's Little Helpers, Allendale Mounted Baseball Club. "The Allendale Mounted Baseball Club, with a team of 150 players," Robert snorted. "First time anyone ever played ball on horseback, with guns instead of bats."

Tension was high in the state as he planned his return trip to Edgefield. Every day there were reports of riots, killings, home-burnings. Listening to the stories, Hannah pleaded with him not to go.

"I must." Robert remembered a phrase from an earlier day. "It's storming the fortress of prejudice. Showing that colored men have courage as well as white. Anyway"—he tried to sound offhanded—"if I die, it'll be with the harness on."

On the morning that he left they gathered on the piazza to wave good-bye—Hannah, Lydia, Elizabeth, Sarah. Hannah was crying as he walked down the steps, but Lydia, frail old Lydia who had seen so much in her long lifetime, tried for a smile. As the horses headed for the station, he watched his family through the carriage window, wondering if he would ever see them again.

Despite his efforts to make light of Hannah's fears, Robert had prepared carefully for the trip. Traveling in the company of federal marshals and a U.S. election commissioner, he was met at the Edgefield station by a company of soldiers. Mounted men with pistols buckled around their waists soon outnumbered the soldiers, but the Republicans were allowed to hold their meeting without interruption.

Escorted back to the station by his military guard, Robert climbed the train steps with a light heart. But he was not to escape so easily. Just as the train pulled away from the platform, a group of Red Shirts clambered aboard. Drunken and menacing, they lurched along the aisle of the car to crowd around Robert and his companions.

A lanky, red-faced youngster loudly announced, "Gonna take a lock of the General's hair."

Robert thrust clenched fists into his pocket, determined not to reply. The only hope of his little group lay in silence. If they ignored the Red Shirts, perhaps they would move along.

But the red-faced boy had no intention of leaving. "Gonna cut General's hair," he sing-songed. As his companions laughed, he took a Bowie knife from his pocket and wiped the blade on his pants.

Robert felt anger rising. If this youngster dared to touch him—— He planted his feet on the floor of the car, preparing to rise.

Without a word, the marshal sitting next to him took his gun from its holster and laid it in Robert's lap. The drunken boy looked from the knife in his hand to the gun in Robert's. Then he drew back. Turning to his companions, he announced, "General's mad. He don't want his hair cut," and staggered off to the other end of the train.

The next day the Charleston *News and Courier* printed a mocking report of the trip in which the Republicans were pictured as cowards. It was headlined, SEE EDGEFIELD AND THEN DIE!

As Election Day drew near, Robert was optimistic about the outcome of the voting. Despite the Red Shirts' reign of terror, the Republicans had proved that they were not cowards. There was little doubt that the Negroes of South Carolina would turn out in force to vote for Chamberlain and Hayes.

There was only one thing wrong with his calculations. He didn't know the extent of the Edgefield plan which called for terror, violence—and fraud at the polls on Election Day.

"Vote early and often," General Butler advised. Red Shirts rode from poll to poll, voting not once or twice but eighteen and twenty times. Even their friends in Georgia and North Carolina crossed the state lines to vote in South Carolina's election, while thousands of Negroes were kept from the polls by red-shirted armies who blocked the roads and barricaded the polling places.

In Edgefield County, where the Republicans had won easily two years earlier, there was now a large Democratic majority. So large, in fact, that embarrassed election officials reported 2,200 more votes than there were voters. The same thing was true in Laurens, another upstate county where the Red Shirts were strong.

On the day after the election, Robert rode to the station to wait for the Charleston newspapers. When they arrived, the headlines proclaimed a Democratic victory: TILDEN OUR PRESIDENT.

On the following day the papers were less confident. HAMPTON PROBABLY ELECTED GOVERNOR.

Two days later they were reporting, BOTH SIDES STOUTLY CLAIM PRESIDENTIAL PRIZE.

Two more weeks and it was REPUBLICANS STEALING THE STATE.

By the time Robert and Elizabeth returned to Washington in December, there were two governors in South Carolina and editorial writers all over the country were asking, WHO WILL BE PRESIDENT?

*Make me resign when I am innocent, when the only
testimony against me is that of a self-confessed thief?*
Robert Smalls

23. On Trial

The Capitol cloakrooms and corridors were blue with
cigar smoke as excited lawmakers assembled to dis-
cuss the election. The first returns showed a victory
for Tilden. But there were three states—Louisiana,
Florida and South Carolina—where both parties
claimed to have won. If every single electoral vote in
these states was counted for Hayes, then he would enter
the White House.

Robert spent his days in Congress and his nights in
the telegraph office on Massachusetts Avenue keeping in
touch with events at home. In South Carolina, the election board had refused to count the Edgefield and Laurens returns because they had been obtained by fraud.
When this ruling gave the state to the Republicans, the
Democrats organized their own government. Columbia
was divided into two armed camps, with Governor
Chamberlain and the Republicans meeting in the State
House and Governor Hampton and the Democrats assembled in a nearby hall. Federal troops guarded the

State House and Red Shirts patrolled the streets near the Democratic legislature. At any moment it seemed as if the Civil War were about to begin all over again.

.. With similar contests in Florida and Louisiana, where there were also two governors and two legislatures, who in Washington was to decide how to count the electoral votes? If it were left up to the Senate, where the Republicans had a majority, then Hayes would be elected. If it were up to the House, which was Democrat-controlled, then Tilden would be President.

The questions to be decided on were of such grave importance that Robert remained in Washington even when a telegram from Hannah informed him of his mother's death. In her eighty-eighth year, Lydia had died in her sleep, died peacefully with a smile on her face.

Elizabeth went home for the funeral, returning to sit in the crowded visitors' gallery of the House on the day that her father accused South Carolina's Democrats "of turning the day of election into a carnival of bloodshed and violence, of violating the purity of the ballot box by unblushing fraud." At the conclusion of his speech he read letters from Republican electors who had been offered fifty thousand dollars if they would switch their votes to Tilden.

All winter long, the Smalls heard rumors of similar bribes that were being offered and deals arranged. The electoral contest was not being settled in Congress, but in smoke-filled rooms in Wormley's Hotel and in the parlors along Pennsylvania Avenue. And it was not the Democrats alone who were offering bribes. The Republicans were wooing their old enemies in the South with promises of railroads, federal funds for state improvements, cabinet posts—and more, if they would vote for Hayes.

At the end of January, Robert was sure of victory. "I feel that Hayes is bound to be sustained," he wrote to Governor Chamberlain, "which means the success of your government."

It was another month before he learned the truth, learned the full extent of the compromise between the Republicans of the North and the Democrats of the South. In return for Hayes' election, the South was to receive railroads, federal money, cabinet posts—and recognition of the Democratic governors of South Carolina and Louisiana.

Robert could scarcely believe it, but a month after Hayes entered the White House, U.S. troops were withdrawn from South Carolina. Without their support, Governor Chamberlain was forced to resign, leaving Wade Hampton as Governor and General Butler—Butler of Hamburg and Edgefield—as one of South Carolina's Senators.

Returning home after Hayes' inauguration, Robert found Beaufort in a turmoil. Every day hundreds of families were arriving in the city, driven from Edgefield and other upstate counties because they had voted Republican. Hannah had opened the doors of their home to the refugees and the house on Prince Street was crowded to capacity with needy people for whom land and work must be found.

"Makes me think of the freedmen who followed Sherman during the war," Hannah sighed. "Only then there was hope. Now it's all over. It won't be long before they're after us too."

"No." Robert refused to accept defeat. "We're not beaten yet."

"Sam says we can still win in the next election."
Elizabeth joined the discussion. "Sam says——"

"Sam says—Sam says," her father teased. "Seems
to me we've been hearing a lot of what Sam says lately."

Sam was Samuel Bampfield, a graduate of Lincoln
University in Pennsylvania. He had worked with Smalls
during the election campagin and was now clerk of
the court in Beaufort. Sam was saying many things to
Elizabeth, and not all of them were concerned with
politics. It wasn't long before he had something to say
to Robert.

"Liz and I, we want to get married. That is," he
corrected himself, "may we have your permission?"

Robert beamed. Sam was one of the postwar generation of educated Negroes whom he counted on to take
leadership in South Carolina. He was almost as proud
of young Bampfield as he was of his daughter. Con-
senting to the wedding, he invited the young couple to
live on Prince Street until they could buy a home of
their own.

While Hannah and Elizabeth traveled up to Charleston to shop for a trousseau and wedding gown, the
political scene grew steadily darker. The Hampton government cut school funds in half. Negro students and
teachers were dismissed from the state university and
the prison reforms of reconstruction were abandoned.
In a short time there were only a handful of Negro
judges, jurors and election officials.

Anyone less optimistic than Robert might well have
seen cause for discouragement. But he was still Congressman Smalls, still the representative of South Carolina's "Black District," where Negroes outnumbered
whites by five to one. In the dark days of 1877, he had

never been more popular at home. There was a story going the rounds about two Sea Islanders who met at a crossroads store.

"I tell you Smalls is the greatest man in the world," the first man said.

"Yes, he's great," his companion admitted, "but not the greatest."

"Then who's greater than Smalls?"

"Why, Jesus Christ."

"Oh," the first man said, "Smalls is young yet."

Smalls was popular and Smalls was prosperous and as an individual he had no cause to worry. Or so it seemed in the summer of 1877. By fall he was not so sure.

One of the first acts of the Hampton government was to appoint a committee to investigate Republican corruption. They hoped to prove to the world that the bloodshed and cheating that had won them the election was all in the good cause of reform.

For months the state was treated to the spectacle of men admitting to bribetaking and bribegiving and all kinds of thievery and rascality. The worst rascals shouted the loudest about how badly they had behaved.

The worst rascal of them all was Josephus Woodruff, a white South Carolinian who had been clerk of the state Senate and head of the company that did the state's printing. In the first years of reconstruction he made money hand over fist; under Chamberlain, his printing bills had been cut in half, and in half again. Now he was the investigating committee's chief witness. From a little black notebook filled with shorthand notes, he read name after name of state assemblymen whom he'd bribed.

"But why is he confessing to so much?" Hannah asked. "He's given enough evidence against himself for them to put him in jail for the rest of his life."

Robert's laugh was bitter. "He's working for the Democrats now for the same reason he worked for us —because it's to his own best interest. He was clerk of the Senate under the Republicans and he's clerk of the Senate under the Democrats. Joe'll never go to jail."

Josephus Woodruff didn't go to jail, but Robert Smalls did. A week before he was due back in Washington for the opening of Congress, a deputy marshal arrived on Prince Street with a warrant for his arrest. He was charged with accepting a five thousand dollar bribe from Josephus Woodruff in 1873.

He traveled up to Columbia in handcuffs, to be released on bail the following day. In Columbia, he had some interesting visitors. The first was John Cochran, chairman of the investigating committee.

"Smalls, you had better resign," Cochran advised.

"Resign what?"

"Resign your seat in Congress."

"What?" Robert pretended not to understand. "The seat the people elected me to?"

"You had better resign," Cochran repeated, "because if you don't they are going to convict you."

Robert shook his head. "I don't believe it. I'm innocent and they can't do it."

"They can do it." There was an edge to Cochran's voice. "They have the court and they have the jury. An indictment is a conviction."

Next came Mr. Drayton, a newspaper editor from Aiken County. "Smalls, we don't want to harm you. We know you were kind to our people just after the surrender and Governor Hampton says he doesn't want to injure you. But we want this government and we intend to have it.

"If you'll vacate your office," Drayton continued, "we'll pay you ten thousand dollars for your two years' salary."

By this time Robert was indignant. The same men who were accusing him of bribetaking were now offering him a bribe.

"If you want me to resign," he angrily replied, "you must call meetings all over the Congressional district and get the people who elected me to pass resolutions requiring me to resign. Then you can have the office without a penny. Otherwise, I'd suffer myself to go to the penitentiary and rot before I'd resign because of a trumped-up charge."

Drayton left, flushed with anger, and Robert knew that he was in for serious trouble. While he was awaiting trial he went to Washington to take his seat in the House. A handful of Congressmen led by Benjamin Butler, the same Butler who had coined the word "contraband" when he was a general during the war, met to see what they could do in his behalf.

South Carolina newspapers, headlining THE DOWNFALL OF SMALLS and THE CULPRIT CONGRESSMAN, had already judged him guilty. One paper pointed out that he had stolen the *Planter,* while another said that the ship had been delivered to the Union by a fellow named Jenkins, whom Smalls had robbed of fame. In either case, he was a thief and ought to be convicted.

With little hope for a fair trial in the state, Congressman Butler drew up a petition asking that the Smalls case be heard in a United States court. "Great prejudice exists against him," the petition pointed out, "so that he cannot have a fair and impartial trial by reason of political excitement and by reason of prejudices excited against him by articles published in the newspapers."

Armed with the petition, Robert returned to Columbia. Of all the men whose misdeeds had been reported to the investigating committee, only two others had been arrested: Francis Cardozo, former state Treasurer and a leader in the reform movement during reconstruction, and Cass Carpenter, a white newspaper editor who had exposed the Ku-Klux Klan. A jury quickly found them "Guilty as charged."

Then came "The State against Robert Smalls." Butler's petition to move the case to a United States court was denied. Smalls' motion to discharge the case because it was a conspiracy to keep him from his seat in Congress was refused. The jury solemnly filed into their seats and Josephus Woodruff took the witness stand. Basing his testimony on the notes in his little black book, shorthand notes that no one else could read, he testified that he had given Smalls a $5,000 check. The check was never produced, nor were there any witnesses to the transaction except Woodruff, a man who admitted robbing the state of $250,000.

"A systematic, constitutional, hereditary, wool-dyed liar," Smalls' lawyer called him, "who is purchasing immunity by testifying in these cases."

The testimony didn't matter. Smalls' denial didn't matter. The verdict of guilty was a foregone conclusion and all that remained was to learn the sentence. Cardozo and Carpenter had been given two years in the county jail when Robert was ordered to stand and face the crowded court.

In a harsh voice, the judge announced, "The sentence of this court is that the defendant, Robert Smalls, be confined at hard labor in the state penitentiary for three years."

Not the county jail, along with Cardozo and Carpenter, but three years in the state penitentiary! Once the reconstruction government had abolished whipping posts and the system of contract labor whereby prisoners were leased out to private farmers. Their laws had been repealed and the whipping post was on its way back, along with iron collars and ankle chains and a treadmill like the one in Ryan's jail. Three years in the penitentiary meant a return to a slavery far worse than any that Robert had ever known.

Suddenly all of his optimism oozed away. He was dazed as he followed a marshal to his cell. When Hannah visited him a few days later she found him sitting on his cot with his head in his hands, too miserable to talk. It was Thanksgiving Day and she'd brought him a turkey dinner.

"Don't feel like eating," he mumbled.

Don't feel like talking. Don't feel like eating. This broken, beaten man didn't seem like the Robert she knew. She told him so, scolding as she might have scolded Elizabeth or Sarah.

"Did you do anything wrong?"

He shook his head.

"Then why are you hiding your face?"

He sighed heavily. "Ma always said, 'Pride goes before a fall.' I was too sure of myself, too sure everything would turn out right."

"Pride got nothing to do with it," Hannah persisted. "At least not the way you mean. Maybe you should be proud they gave you the worst sentence.

Shows that of all the men in the state they fear you the most."

Robert didn't answer, but he was listening closely as Hannah continued. "Everyone on the islands is up in arms. Even the white men say the Governor should step in."

His shoulders slowly straightened as she told of the Beaufort merchants who were raising his ten thousand dollars bail and of his lawyer's plan to appeal the case.

"Appeal'll lose," he pointed out.

"Probably," she agreed, "but then he'll take it to the Supreme Court."

By this time he was nodding thoughtfully, estimating his chances before the nine black-robed judges in Washington. Before she left he was pacing the cell, waving a turkey leg in his hand as he dictated a note for Congressman Butler.

Released on bail before the week was out, he returned to his seat in the House. The case dragged on. More than a year went by before his appeal was turned down in the state court and he was able to tell his story in the highest court in the land. While he waited his turn on the Supreme Court's crowded calendar, he was astonished to receive a letter from the Governor of South Carolina granting a "full and free pardon to the said Robert Smalls."

Without his knowledge, a deal had been made between State Attorney-General Youmans and the U. S. District Attorney. If the United States would drop its cases against South Carolinians accused of violating election laws, then South Carolina would drop its charges against the reconstruction leaders.

Instead of being pleased, Robert was angry. Calling meetings in Beaufort and Columbia, he denounced the

Governor's action. It meant freedom, he explained, but not vindication. People would still be able to say, "There goes Smalls, the convicted thief."

Despite the pardon, he determined to carry on his Supreme Court fight. Only a few days later he learned that Attorney-General Youmans was in Washington, asking the Supreme Court to drop the Smalls case because it had been settled in South Carolina. He sent off an urgent telegram to his lawyer:

"I see by the papers that Youmans has moved to strike my case from the docket. Stop it. There is a principle involved. My right is involved."

Hastily throwing some clothes into a suitcase, he boarded the next train for the North. But he was too late. While he was changing trains in Charleston, a messenger handed him a wire from Washington.

"Case stricken off yesterday."

Disappointed though he was, Robert managed a wry grin when he learned that the State of South Carolina had been so eager to drop the case that Youmans had paid to Robert's lawyer the $125 he had spent in bringing it to court. The grin turned to a smile of satisfaction the following week when another letter from the Governor arrived. The Governor was commissioning him as captain in the state militia "for meritorious service rendered."

The commission was intended as an apology, but for the rest of his political life Robert was to hear himself spoken of as a bribetaker and ex-convict. It was not until 1895 that the Charleston *News and Courier,* stern critic of reconstruction and Smalls, spoke in his defense. Ignoring their stories of earlier years, the editors reported:

"It is a simple statement of fact to stay that he was

tried at a time and under circumstances that did not tend to assure him a fair trial and that not a few white men in Columbia who attended his trial held the evidence offered to be insufficient to convict him. The action of the jury has been the subject of criticism and remark in Columbia from that day to this, and we believe it safe to say that he could not be convicted before a jury of impartial white men anywhere on the same evidence today."

> *"This, Mr. Chairman, is perhaps the Negroes' tempo-rary farewell to the American Congress; but let me say, Phoenix-like he will rise up some day and come again."*
>
> George H. White, last Negro
> Congressman from the South, 1901

24. *"The End of Smalls"*

Re-elected to Congress despite his arrest, Robert spent the better part of each year in Washington. After Lydia's death, he begged Hannah to join him in the capital city, but she was reluctant to leave Beaufort.

"I'm too old to be uprooted now," she protested. "My home is here."

Occasionally she boarded a train for the North, to attend an inaugural ball or a White House tea for Congressmen's wives, but during most of Robert's years in the House, Sarah was his companion. While acting as her father's part-time secretary, she finished high school and went on to normal school in Washington.

Accompanied by his daughter, Robert was a familiar figure at Presidential receptions and Sunday at-homes. A conservative dresser, he never appeared without the Prince Albert suit, top hat and high-buttoned shoes that the fashion of the time prescribed. Grown stout, with white whiskers and trim goatee, he was a perfect picture of a Congressman of distinction. It was hard for acquaintances to remember his slave origins.

Outside of official functions, most of his leisure was spent in the Negro society of the city. In the last quarter of the 19th century, Washington was home for many of the country's Negro leaders, men like Blanche Bruce, U. S. Senator from Mississippi, Frances Cardozo, now principal of a District of Columbia high school, and Smalls' boyhood idol, Frederick Douglass.

Robert renewed his acquaintance with Miss Forten-who-knows-everything, who had married Reverend Francis Grimke, pastor of the Fifteenth Street Presbyterian Church. He spoke alongside Frederick Douglass at Emancipation Day banquets and debated at the Bethel Literary Society, where Douglass and Cardozo were also members.

When the G.A.R., the organization of Union Civil War veterans celebrated the twentieth anniversary of the capture of the *Planter,* he traveled to Boston as their guest of honor. He was greeted by the Mayor, entertained by Governor Long at the State House— and refused a room at Boston's leading hotel.

There were balls and teas, concerts and debates— and long evenings of euchre in the Smalls' rooms on L Street, when trayloads of crabs and gallons of cider were consumed. "General Smalls is a genial host, a first-rate gentleman and a good judge of cider," a Washington newspaper reported. "He entertained last Monday night at his handsomely furnished parlors in a manner which will not soon be forgotten. There is nothing small about Smalls."

In Congress he continued to speak for all the people in his district, presenting a petition for women suffrage from the ladies of Beaufort and a bill for the relief of farmers, fighting for pensions for Negro soldiers and payments to Confederate planters who had lost their lands in the war. Close to his heart was a bill to restore the books taken from the Beaufort library by the Union in 1862. Although he asked for the return of the books and five thousand dollars to replace those that had been lost, Congress did not grant the request until 1940.

Now that he was no longer a freshman Congressman, he was able to win support for bills for the improvement of South Carolina harbors and the establishment of a naval station on Port Royal Bay. The naval station proved to be one of his major accomplishments in Congress. Located on Parris Island, it was later taken over by the Marine Corps and is still the Marines' basic training center on the Atlantic coast and an important source of income for the citizens of Beaufort and Hilton Head.

When Robert first entered the House, there were eight Negroes in Congress. By 1881 their numbers had dwindled to two and he found himself representing not only South Carolina, but the members of his race everywhere. If a Negro was discriminated against in a restaurant or forced to sit in the Jim Crow cars that were beginning to make their appearance on Southern railroads, he wrote to *his* Congressman, Robert Smalls. If a Negro planned to bring his family on a visit to the capital at Easter, he wrote to *his* Congressman, and Sarah spent much of her time making hotel reservations and arranging for White House tours. If a Negro wanted a government job, he wrote to Robert, or, more often than not, arrived at the Smalls' parlor door with a suitcase and a list of his qualifications.

On the floor of the House, Robert argued against segregation. "In Georgia they have a car called a second-class car," he said. "Notwithstanding, a colored man may buy a first-class ticket here in Washington, yet when he reaches the State of Georgia, he is compelled to go into a 'Jim Crow car' which is placed next to the locomotive."

He spoke up for pay raises for Negro employees at Annapolis and for the men who worked in the House cloakroom. One of his best known speeches was a plea for a pension for the widow of General David Hunter, whose memory, he said, was "dear to every colored man's heart."

Back home between sessions of Congress he was Beaufort's leading citizen. Whenever travelers visited the state they sought him out as a "representative man." Sir George Campbell, a member of the British Parliament, toured the Sea Islands in his company, noting in his journal, "General Smalls seems to be on very popular and pleasant terms with the people. They all salute him heartily and ask him all kinds of questions and he has always something to say to them."

When ex-President and Mrs. Grant were returning to the North from Florida, they stopped at Beaufort. Met at the Station by the Smalls' carriage, they were escorted to their hotel by the Beaufort Light Infantry, the Negro militia company which Robert captained. Standing on the piazza of the Sea Island Hotel, General Grant saluted the parading militia men while Mrs. Grant talked to Hannah and held Julia Bampfield, the first Smalls grandchild, in her arms.

The reception for the Grants was one of the last times Hannah appeared in public. Taken ill one day while she was visiting Elizabeth, she spent bedridden months at home, closing her eyes for the last time on a sultry afternoon in July in 1883.

In the dark days that followed, Robert found himself leaning more and more on Sarah. His "Union baby," now approaching her twentieth birthday, had much of her mother's calm wisdom. No more than five feet tall even when she pinned her hair in a Psyche knot on top of her head, she had a way of saying, "Now, Pa," and suggesting a course of action that lifted his spirits and made him forget despair.

The summer of Hannah's death came to its weary end at last and by fall he was back in harness, ready for the challenge of an election campaign. Elections in South Carolina were still stormy. For years Robert was unable to travel outside of his district without an armed guard; during several campaigns he came close to losing his life.

The closest call of all came when Hannah was still alive. Scheduled to speak in Gillisonville in the western part of his district, he had barely mounted the speaker's stand when a company of Red Shirts rode into town. "Eight hundred of them, pouring into town, whooping like Indians," he said.

Squads of men galloped up and down the street, giving the Rebel yell. Leaning from their saddles, they "licked off the hats" of colored men and slapped the faces of women who were on their way to the meeting. Reining his horse at the speaker's stand, their leader demanded half of Robert's speaking time.

"No," Robert decided. "Then we'll have no meeting."

"There'll be a meeting," the Red Shirt snapped, "and you'll speak alongside us."

When Robert continued to refuse, he was given ten minutes in which to change his mind. Withdrawing into a store with forty of his supporters, he laid careful battle plans. His men were armed and he placed them behind the counters.

"Aim at the door," he ordered. "Keep your finger on your trigger, but don't shoot unless they break in."

When the ten minutes were up there was a scuffle outside. A man shouted, "Open up or we'll burn down the building."

It wasn't long before bullets were raining in through the windows and walls and Robert's men were begging for a chance to shoot back. Under his orders, they held their fire while the people who had come to the meeting spread the alarm.

"Robert Smalls is trapped in a store, surrounded by Red Shirts." "Robert Smalls' life is in danger." By late afternoon every colored man and woman for miles around was running to the rescue with guns, axes, hoes and clubs. A thousand Negroes were on their way to defend him when the Red Shirts thought it best to withdraw.

They galloped away, leaving behind a detachment of armed men to meet the train which Robert would take back to Beaufort. Warned of the ambush, he circled the station and rode to the outskirts of town. In the dark of the evening, he jumped onto the train's tender as it passed. At every station on the way back home he was met by crowds of Negroes who had gathered to make sure that he was safe.

As more and more of the state offices fell into their hands, South Carolina's respectable men began to be embarrassed by the trigger-happy Red Shirts. They decided to put away their guns and win elections by legal means. New laws made it difficult for Negroes to register and almost impossible for them to vote. A black farmer had to travel fifty miles to sign the voting list; a white farmer received his registration certificate in the mail. Voting places in areas where Negroes were in a majority never opened on Election Day. Republican ballots were lost, destroyed and counted out. Democratic ballots were counted over and over again.

Ten years after the election of 1876 there were scarcely any Negro votes in South Carolina—except in Beaufort County. Ten years after the election of 1876 there were no Negro Congressmen from South Carolina —except Robert Smalls. Ten years after the election of 1876, South Carolina's leaders resolved to put an end to the "Black District" in their otherwise lily-white state.

In the weeks before the election, every newspaper predicted "The End of Smalls." Every Democrat, from President Cleveland down to the lowliest district leader, was hard at work for his opponent, William Elliott, an ex-Confederate colonel. Men and money poured into Beaufort and an army of speakers pleaded, cajoled, thundered, "The all-important thing is to beat the convict Smalls."

Robert shrugged off the propaganda barrage. He was still holding meetings on Bay Street with Allen's Brass Band playing and an enthusiastic audience singing:

> *"Elliot rides the milk-white horse.*
> *Cleveland rides the lamb.*
> *Smalls doesn't ride anything at all,*
> *But he gets there just the same."*

Beloved by the Negroes ("The men, women and children seem to regard him with a feeling akin to worship," the *News and Courier* said), he was also assured of the votes of many of Beaufort's white men.

There were 32,000 Negro voters in his district and 7,000 white. The Democrats couldn't count him out. They couldn't—but they did. By "legal" means, they kept 25,000 colored men from the polls. Then by "legal" means, they threw out all of the votes cast on Lady's Island, St. Helena and in Beaufort, in order to give a majority to his opponent. It was as simple as that.

"They tell you that my vote has fallen off, that my people have gone against me. They say that I have become unpopular," Robert said. "No sir, no vote has fallen off. The vote is the same today and more, but Democrats have improved their methods of preventing votes from getting into the box."

Even some newspapers agreed with him. Calling the election "a bold theft, a miserable blunder, and a moral wrong," the Greenville, South Carolina, *News* said, "We doubt if there has ever been a more unwise or absurd proceeding than the fight against Smalls and the methods used in making it. The state will be put before the country as being party to a plain, deliberate and wanton fraud."

Robert went to work immediately to contest the election. With a team of lawyers, he traveled through the district, talking to men who had not been permitted to vote or whose votes were not counted. After spending many months and many thousands of dollars, he was prepared to prove that he had won. He could prove this by the sworn statements of thousands of witnesses—if Congress would listen to him.

In the past, Congress had acted quickly in deciding contested elections, but the eight hundred pages of testimony in the case of Smalls vs. Elliott were allowed to gather dust on committee-room shelves for more than a year. It was not until the last month of the session that Smalls' evidence was brought before the House.

Everyone realized that the debate involved more than Robert Smalls' seat. For the first time since reconstruction began there were no Negro Congressmen in Washington. Beyond the case of Smalls vs. Elliott was the broader question of whether Negroes in the South were to have the right to vote and to elect representatives to Congress.

The Southerners who controlled the Committee on Elections concentrated their fire on Robert. He was pictured as an ex-convict, a bribetaker who instituted a reign of terror in order to keep colored men from voting for Colonel Elliott.

Allowed an hour to answer their charges, he marshalled every scrap of evidence he had collected in his defense. Somehow it was not good enough. His heart sank as he looked around the familiar chamber, noting the indifferent faces, listening to the halfhearted applause.

There was time for one last appeal. "I would ask you, gentlemen, after you have cast your votes against me, to take this record home and in your leisure moments read the testimony. When you get through you will say to yourselves, 'I have done one Negro a wrong in my life.' If you could only stop with saying 'one.'"

Perhaps he jolted his audience more than he thought. For a day, for two days, the House's leading Republicans rose to speak in his defense. There was

Henry Cabot Lodge of Massachusetts, who in the following years was to fight a losing battle for a national election law, Rowell of Illinois, Johnston of Indiana, McComas of Maryland, La Follette of Wisconsin.

Young Bob La Follette, at the beginning of a distinguished political career, spoke most forcefully. "Confused, baffled, discouraged, cheated, the colored vote of the South has quietly and speedily disappeared from the returns," he reminded his listeners. "The new election methods of the South have done their perfect work.

"You say in justification that the Negro is ignorant, inferior, incapable of growth. Secretly, do you not fear the opposite? Is it against the dull and submissive that you direct your hardest blows? Or are they aimed at those who, like Robert Smalls, have shown intellect, courage and determination to lift their people to a higher level and maintain their rights as free men?"

He pleaded with his colleagues. "Give to General Robert Smalls, whose distinguished services for the Union, whose skill as a political organizer and courage as a defender of the civil rights of his race early marked him for persecution; give to this old man, this old soldier, the seat to which he was honestly elected."

In a final burst of oratory, he offered to "lie down and beg for that justice to which every man in the House knows he is entitled."

There were cries of "Vote, Vote," and a motion was passed and seconded: "That Robert Smalls was elected and is entitled to a seat in the 50th Congress." But when the count was in there were 127 Yeas and 142 Nays —and Robert Smalls' Congressional career was at an end.

*The only thing that we can do as patriots and states-
men is to take from them every ballot that we can
under the laws of the national government.*

Benjamin Tillman, 1895

25. The Clock Turns Back

It was a blustery February day and even in South Carolina there was a hint of snow in the air when Robert
returned from Washington. Sarah and Elizabeth were
waiting for him at the station.

Sarah forced a smile. "What now, Poppa?" she
asked.

What now? Robert was fifty years old and today
he felt like the "old man" of La Follette's speech. His
life had been full—and now it was empty. Without
Hannah, without his work in Congress, what was there
to look forward to?

He had his daughters and a growing number of
grandchildren in the Bampfield house on North Street.
He had his horses, Ethan Allen, a thoroughbred pacer,
and Major Beaufort, a trotter who regularly won
prizes at county fairs. He had his home with its neatly
trimmed hedges and its white-paneled rooms. But
children, houses, horses, these were no substitutes for
life.

214

"A man must work." He was rocking in his favorite chair on the piazza after dinner. "A man must have something to work for."

"But, sir"—Sam Bampfield was sitting on the top step with his arms folded around his knees—"they say its always darkest before the dawn. We still have men in the state legislature. We still control most of the county offices. The fact is——"

"The fact is," Robert interrupted, "that for the first time in my life I must look for a job. In the last two years the lawyers managed to use up all my savings."

"I'm working, Pa. I'll support you." There was a twinkle in Sarah's eyes as she joined the conversation. She was teaching in the school on Carteret Street for a salary of twenty-five dollars a month.

Robert smiled fondly at her. "You don't earn enough money to keep your piano in tune."

"But there are my music lessons too. I have quite a few pupils."

"She's going to have a recital in May. Wait till you see how nicely those children play and dance." Elizabeth, too, was trying to cheer up her father.

"Seriously, sir, if you need any money——" Sam left his offer dangling in mid-air.

Touched, Robert hastened to reassure him. "Things are not that bad. There are rents coming in from my houses. Afraid I'm just feeling old today. Being beaten, it's hard on a man."

As the weeks went by his defeat became less painful. Early in April a letter from Senator John Sherman asked if he would be interested in the position of Collector of Customs for Beaufort. The businessmen of the town signed a petition urging his appointment and in June it was confirmed by President Harrison. This time his return from Washington was triumphant, with Allen's Brass Band booming out a welcome at the station and a crowd of well-wishers waiting to congratulate him.

Two days later he hung up his hat in the red-brick building on Bay Street which long ago had housed Captain Elwell and the Army Quartermaster Corps. From his office in the rear of the building he could see the ships at anchor in the bay, awaiting his clearance before loading or unloading cargo.

After the war, phosphates had been discovered in the rivers along the coast and Beaufort was a busy port, exporting cotton and lumber as well as the valuable fertilizer rock. With two deputies, a boatman and a messenger, Smalls collected customs fees and kept records of the merchant vessels as they entered and left the harbor. His salary wasn't high—less than two thousand dollars a year—but he resolved to become the most efficient customs collector that the Treasury Department had ever seen.

He had work, but he still needed something to work for. As the summer drew to a close, Sarah noticed that he was making frequent trips to Charleston.

"Twice last month and now it's every weekend," she confided in Elizabeth. "Could it be—course it couldn't be—that Poppa's courting?"

At Christmas time they knew the answer when Miss Annie Wigg, a Charleston school teacher, arrived to spend the holidays on Prince Street. Only two years older than Elizabeth, Annie was gentle, handsome, gay. Robert's face came alive again as he watched her dance the schottische and heard her sing his favorite songs. She made friends quickly with his daughters, and even Pa John, his groom, had a special smile for her when he drove the barouche to the boat landing at the end of the holiday week.

The jessamine bushes were yellow and the fat buds of the magnolias just beginning to unfold when the citizens of Beaufort, black and white together, crowded into the Baptist church to witness the wedding of Annie Wigg and Robert Smalls. Two small Bampfield girls acted as bridesmaids and a friend wrote a ballad to celebrate the occasion:

> *They gather in his lovely home,*
> *At Beaufort's ocean side,*
> *His friends and guests, to wish him joy*
> *And see his winning bride.*

> *We wish them all the blessings*
> *That mortal lot befalls,*
> *Prosperity and length of days,*
> *General and Mrs. Smalls.*

The years seemed to drop from Robert's shoulders as he and Annie sailed in the harbor on sunny weekends and swam and picnicked on the sandy island beaches. Even the old house grew young again. A crew of workmen added an upstairs piazza on the front and a bedroom on the rear. There were new draperies at the windows and new pictures on the walls. In the parlor Annie hung portraits of Robert's Civil War "greats"—Admiral du Pont, General Sherman and General Grant—and her own pastels of Sarah and the *Planter*.

Two years later, in 1892, there was another addition to the household, a son whom Annie named William Robert. Willie was a plump and healthy baby, soon creeping down the piazza steps to explore the yard, and his father's happiness was complete.

"Soldier, sailor, tinker, tailor." Robert counted the buttons on his son's pinafore. "What kind of a man are you going to be, anyway?"

Shaking his head at the baby's chuckles of delight, he grew serious. "What kind of world will you live to see?"

Willie would face a different world than his sisters had grown up in. The old dreams of freedom and equality were fast fading away for Negroes in the South. There were fewer and fewer Negro voters, fewer and fewer Negro lawmakers, and the funds for Negro schools were only a third of those for white schools. A white man accused of a crime against a Negro was sure of acquittal. A Negro accused of a crime against a white man was sure to be convicted—if he was not lynched before being brought to trial.

The situation had grown worse each year, and there was still more to come. Soon after the Smalls' marriage, Benjamin Tillman of Edgefield had been elected Governor of the state. "Pitchfork Ben" was a one-eyed, fierce-looking man who boasted that he was the founder of South Carolina's first Red Shirt club. On his parlor mantelpiece he proudly displayed the rifle that he had used in the Hamburg massacre.

Robert had campaigned vigorously against him, urging the people of his district "to do anything that is legitimate to bring about the defeat of this arch-enemy." Tillman had failed to carry Beaufort County, but he had been elected Governor by a large upstate majority. In his inaugural address he reminded his audience:

"The whites have absolute control of the state

218

government and we intend at all hazards to retain it. We deny that all men are created equal; it is not true now and was not true when Jefferson wrote it."

Perhaps his defeat in Beaufort rankled. At any rate he was determined to banish the last black face from state affairs. To accomplish this he fought for a constitutional convention to revise the 1868 constitution and finally and forever establish South Carolina as "a white man's government." There would be no more violence at the polls, no more ballot-stuffing and ballot-stealing, no more "legal" election laws. By a simple stroke of the pen, a new constitution could eliminate the Negro voter.

In September, 1895, when Willie was three years old, Robert took the train to Columbia to attend the constitutional convention. He left home reluctantly. Annie was feeling poorly and he hated to leave her, but this might be his last opportunity to make his voice heard in South Carolina.

He was one of the two delegates to the convention who had also attended the convention of '68. This time the meeting was held in the State House, with a Confederate flag above the speaker's desk and the original articles of secession framed on the wall. This time there were 154 white delegates and 6 Negroes, five of them from Beaufort. In 1868, the hands of the clock had pointed toward progress. Now they were turning backward at a dizzy pace and there seemed no way to stop them.

Tillman's plan to end Negro voting was "the most charming piece of mechanism ever invented," he said. In addition to the usual residence requirements and the payment of poll taxes, every voter would have to prove that he could read, write, or understand the constitution.

Robert jumped to his feet as soon as he heard the proposal. "To embody such a provision in the election law would mean that every white man would interpret it right," he pointed out, "and every Negro would interpret it wrong."

With a pleased smile, Tillman agreed with him. "There's no particle of fraud or illegality in it," he said. "It's just simply showing partiality, perhaps, or discriminating."

As he listened to the laughter that greeted Tillman's remark, Robert knew that he was fighting a losing battle. Nevertheless, he was determined to state his case.

He spoke again and again, poking fun at George Tillman, his old opponent. "I heard him make a very eloquent speech, but before he got through he had acted like the good Jersey cow which gave her two gallons of milk, and, though she did not put her foot in it, she had shaken so much dirt from her tail into the pail that we could not accept the milk."

He challenged Ben Tillman to change the election law, making education the only qualification for voting so that it would apply to whites as well as Negroes. "Let us make a constitution that is fair, honest and just," he urged. "Let us make a constitution for all of the people."

"Talk about adopting a suffrage plan that will secure a fair and honest election is the talk of a child," a delegate from Berkeley answered. "I tell you, gentlemen, if we have fair elections in Berkeley we can't carry it. The black man is learning to read faster than the white man. We are perfectly disgusted with hearing so much about fair elections. Talk all around, but make it fair and you'll see what'll happen."

The debate was becoming embarrassing. Northern reporters in the crowded gallery of the hall wrote of the "brilliant moral victories" that were being won by the Negro delegates, "the victory of black mind over white matter." "It is not Negro ignorance, but Negro intelligence that is feared," the New York *Press* explained.

Even a white delegate rose to ask, "What oppressed people ever sent a delegation anywhere who in their deportment, in their power of reasoning, in their rhetorical ability, in their knowledge of the law of the land, could surpass in ability that colored delegation from Beaufort?"

There were too many moral victories. Sprawled in his chair with his feet on his desk and his one fierce eye focused on the Beaufort delegation, Ben Tillman made up his mind to attack. Raising the old cries of extravagance and corruption in reconstruction times, he reminded his listeners and the reporters in the gallery of Smalls' convict past.

Robert flushed with anger. In his hand he had a letter from Sarah. Annie was worse. The doctor wasn't sure what was wrong, but thought he should return home immediately. He had planned to ask for a leave of absence, but now, in the face of this unprecedented personal assault, he couldn't go.

Thrusting Sarah's letter in his pocket, he took the floor. Carefully he reviewed the history of his trial, conviction, pardon. In a ringing voice, he summed up:

"My race needs no special defense. All they need is an equal chance in the battle of life. I am proud of them, and by their acts toward me I know that they are not ashamed of me, for they have at all times honored me with their votes."

He sat down to a sprinkling of applause. One more day until the vote was taken and then he could go home to Annie. One more day and the new election law passed by a vote of 77 to 41. As the result was being announced, a page handed him a telegram. His fingers trembled as he tore open the envelope. It was from Sarah.

"Annie died this morning."

Annie dead! Blinded by tears, he stumbled from his seat to catch the next train to Beaufort.

Sarah, careworn, grief-stricken, threw herself into his arms as he opened the front gate. Wordlessly, she led him upstairs to Willie, who was sobbing in the clothes hamper in the hall, refusing to climb out until Poppa arrived. Somehow, he never knew how, he managed to live through the funeral and the sympathy calls and return to Columbia.

Red-eyed and dejected, he once more took his seat in the convention. The election law had passed, but there were other battles to be fought. Many delegates objected to spending money for Negro schools. "I don't intend to erect an educational barrier to the Negro with one hand and tear it down with the other," Ben Tillman frankly stated.

Resolution after resolution supported by the colored delegates were defeated. No compulsory education. No free textbooks. No "mixing of the races" in schools. No popular election of school trustees which would permit Negro school boards in Negro neighborhoods. School taxes were raised but nothing in the new law would prevent most of the money from going to white schools. Robert's only victory was the establishment of a state agricultural and mechanical college for Negroes.

After three months of debate, the constitution was adopted by a vote of 116 to 7. County by county, the delegates marched to the front of the room to fix their signatures to South Carolina's new law. When it was Beaufort's turn, Robert asked, on behalf of the Negro delegates, to be excused.

One man objected. "Any member who doesn't sign shouldn't be paid for his expenses."

"Then I'll walk home," Robert flared back. "I'd rather walk than put my name to a constitution with such an article on suffrage."

County by county, all the delegates except the Beaufort men signed the document. Then a minister led the convention in closing prayer and the delegates sang, "God Be With Us Till We Meet Again." The colored men were silent. When would they ever meet again in South Carolina's State House?

On the train to Beaufort, Robert thought back to '68 and the incredible, hopeful experiment that had begun that year. Then it was spring. Now it was December, cold and dark, and the experiment was ended. Now it was December, cold and dark, and all hope was gone.

"One hundred thousand colored men have been disfranchised in the state. Yet, Senator, you say that there are matters of greater importance before the coming Congress?"

Robert Smalls, 1900

26. When There's Life . . .

"General like to have caved in since Annie died."

The people of Beaufort, rocking on their piazzas, watched Robert walk with bent head and the shuffling step of an old man. He walked without seeing, talked without listening, wandering aimlessly and endlessly from yard to stable, from Prince Street to the Bay and back again.

His home had never seemed so big and so barren. There were days when he felt like a condemned man. Condemned to live for how many more years—ten, twenty? It was an endless stretch of time to spend alone.

But he soon found that he wasn't alone. A small boy crept into his bed one night. A small boy climbed on his knee as he sat by the fire. A small boy listened gravely to his stories of slavery days and the great war.

The big empty house grew noisy and crowded. There

224

were horses in the stable, dogs in the yard, ducks in the pond, and bicycles cluttering up the once-neat path. Al and Lise Bampfield came to play with Willie on the broad piazza and to stay for dinner with Grandpa and Aunt Sarah. After dinner there was music, with Sarah at the piano and Willie singing "Auld Lang Syne" and "Coming Through the Rye," or practicing on the clarinet that Mr. Allen of the brass band was teaching him to play.

At first Robert just went through the motions of living, "so regular you could set your clock by him," a neighbor said. Up at seven when the town bell rang. Breakfast at eight, with an unvarying diet of hominy grits and hot bread or pancakes, never "baker's bread." Promptly at nine the flag was raised in front of the Customs House and the office opened for business. Promptly at noon, Robert left for lunch, a sandwich and malted at the corner drugstore, and a trip to the bank or the dry goods store across the street. Promptly at four, the flag was lowered and he headed for home.

Willie was waiting on the piazza to shout "Here comes Poppa" as a warning to the cook to set out the dinner plates. Dinner might be shrimp mull and rice, deviled crabs, oysters or turkey, with a silver pitcher filled with iced tea or the lime juice that English sea captains brought him when they came to port. "General eats splendidly," an old friend sighed.

At eight-thirty he rose from his chair to close the blinds and shutters and lock the doors. Bedtime was at nine, winter or summer, except when there were visitors.

There were visitors often, neighbors, old political friends, and travelers from the North. All of Beaufort dropped by to admire Sarah's night-blooming cereus when its pale blossoms unfolded on warm nights in fall. At Christmas time the yard was lit up by Roman candles and rockets, to the delight of Willie and the Bampfield boys and girls. On Decoration Day it was the starting-off point and the end of a parade.

Decoration Day, set aside as a day on which to honor Union soldiers, was observed in the South only by the Negroes. Soon after the war Union dead were moved to a National Cemetery on the outskirts of Beaufort. On the thirtieth of May thousands of Negroes from all along the coast traveled by train and excursion steamer to decorate the graves with flowers and flags.

With a ceremonial sword buckled to his waist, Robert led the Beaufort Light Infantry to the cemetery, introduced the speakers—men like Booker T. Washington—and entertained them afterward at his home. In the evening, when the parades and barbecues were over, Allen's Brass Band marched once more to Prince Street to serenade the Smalls and their guests.

Sometimes there were so many visitors that Robert wondered how he could have thought that he would be lonely. One Decoration Day night Sarah called him into the kitchen to whisper in distress, "Pa, we don't have enough cups and saucers."

As he watched the people who were crowding into the parlor, the dining room and the hall, Robert sighed, "We have plenty of cups and saucers. We have too much company."

Walking through the streets of Beaufort where white and black alike leaned on their gateposts to say, "Morning, General. Nice day, isn't it?" or "What are they up to now in Washington?", it was hard to realize how much the South had changed.

The situation had gone from bad to worse to worst. Every one of the former Confederate states had passed election laws similar to South Carolina's. Less votes meant more lynchings—riots, shootings, hangings, burnings in every state. Less votes meant more discrimination—Jim Crow cars on trains, "For Whites Only" signs in public places.

After 1898, when Robert took the train to Columbia he rode in a railroad coach labeled "Colored," a dirty, foul-smelling coach with battered seats and broken windows. In 1904, when he boarded a street car in Charleston he was told to stand in the rear. He left the car at the next corner. It was forty years since he'd been thrown off a street car in Philadelphia and now it was starting all over again.

For a time there was still Negro voting in Beaufort. As late as 1903 he wrote to a friend, "Our municipal election comes here on Monday and as we have never lost an election here since reconstruction, I am anxious to be here on that day." Then even Beaufort was lost. Although Robert continued to vote for the rest of his life he was one of a handful of Negroes who were permitted to do so.

Three or four times a year he traveled to Washington, taking Willie with him to meet President McKinley and President Roosevelt and to sit on the floor during House debates. At first it seemed as if everything were the same in the North. His friends in Congress voted him a pension for his war services and additional prize money for the *Planter,* and his appointment as Collector of Customs was regularly confirmed.

During the Spanish-American War, President Mc-

Kinely invited him to serve as colonel of a Negro regiment; a few years later he was offered the post of Minister to Liberia. In 1900, he traveled to the Middle West to campaign for McKinley's re-election. In 1904, he cast his vote for Theodore Roosevelt at the Republican convention in Chicago. In 1906, he addressed the Harvard University chapter of the Phi Beta Kappa society at the invitation of ex-Governor John Long.

He was still General Smalls, war hero, Republican leader, and he was still talking to the President, writing to Senators, lunching with Congressmen, speaking for his people. "We need a national election law to protect Negro voters." "The South's representation in Congress should be cut down so long as half its citizens are kept from the polls." "Jim Crow cars are unconstitutional." "There ought to be a federal law against lynching."

Everything seemed the same, but it wasn't. He was General of a militia regiment that no longer existed. He was a hero in the war before the last one. He was a leader in a political party that no longer needed him.

Practical politicians weren't interested in voteless voters. Every year the "lily-white" movement was gaining strength in the Republican Party. Every year the Republicans' protests about the treatment of Negroes in the South were growing fainter and fainter until at last they couldn't be heard at all.

There were fewer and fewer government jobs for black Republicans. Once there had been hundreds of Negro postmasters, tax collectors, customs officials. By 1910, Robert was writing, "No, I have not been reappointed as yet, neither do I know of any Negro who has been appointed to office in the South by the present administration." In 1912, a Republican Congress failed to confirm him as Collector of Customs and in June of the following year he went out of office.

The loss of the job no longer mattered to Robert. He was seventy-four years old and the doctors said he had diabetes, for which no cure was known. But he was still fighting. He could no more stop fighting than he could stop breathing.

In the spring of 1913, a white man on St. Helena was killed. Two Negro suspects were locked up in the county jail in Beaufort, awaiting trial, when word reached the Customs House that a mob was forming upstate to lynch them.

Robert, who still kept a loaded rifle in his bedroom, quickly called a council of war. "There's never been a lynching in Beaufort, and there's not going to be one now," he announced.

"How you going to stop it, General?" Henry Garrett, the Customs House boatman, questioned him.

Robert's plan was a bold one. Negroes were to be stationed throughout Beaufort, ready to set fire to white homes if the mob entered the city.

"But burning people's homes, what good'll that do?" Henry protested. "It isn't Beaufort men who are starting the lynching."

"But it's Beaufort men can stop it," Robert said positively, "if they know we mean business."

In an hour's time all of Beaufort knew that General Smalls and his lieutenants "meant business." In an hour's time, the sheriff had sworn in extra deputies. All that night and the next day they stood guard along the highway and at the boat landing. The mob turned back and Beaufort never had its lynching.

In his last years, when he no longer felt well enough to travel, Robert turned more and more often to the school on Carteret Street. Emancipation Day, Decoration Day, and just plain everyday day found him there, speaking at assemblies and wandering through the classrooms and the playground to see if more books or baseball bats were needed.

If Robert ever had a hobby, it was Beaufort's colored school. To the children he was still the greatest man in the world. Little boys imitated his speeches and his portly walk while little girls proudly reported to their mothers, "General was at school today. Told about how he stole the *Planter*."

It was not only about the *Planter* that General talked. He gave the children messages to bring home to their parents. With Beaufort's only newspaper boasting that the county had at last been taken over by "clean white Democrats," the school assembly was one of the few platforms he had left. He talked politics and history, telling them about the Civil War and the days of reconstruction, when anything seemed possible in the best of all possible worlds.

He scolded, too, about the value of an education. "I've done reasonably well for myself. Imagine how much more I could have accomplished if I'd had schooling. Education's here for you, and I ask you to take it."

Across the street from the colored school was the school that Beaufort's white children attended. At recess time colored and white ran and shouted together, crowding around the old woman who came to sell them taffy. To Robert, these children were the future. Through their eyes, he looked ahead to the day when there would be no more lynchings, no more discrimination, no more streets dividing the two races.

But this was a day that he would never see. In June,

1914, Willie came home with a college diploma and a brand-new wife. A wedding reception planned for the young couple was postponed because Robert Smalls had hooked his cane in the rack in the hall and gone to bed. He never got up again. On the twenty-third of February, 1915, when newspapers were headlining a new war across the ocean, he stopped fighting because he stopped breathing.

Robert Smalls had lived his life, lived it fully and lived it well. His funeral was the largest ever seen in Beaufort. Mourners filled the Baptist church to overflowing, and flowers and telegrams poured in from all over the country. When the words of praise had been spoken, the hymns sung, the tears shed, Allen's Brass Band led General on his last parade, a slow procession through the streets of Beaufort to his grave in the churchyard on Craven Street.

More than fifty years have passed since his death. His grandchildren and great grandchildren—school principals, teachers, government workers, doctors' and ministers' wives—are scattered across the nation. Elizabeth celebrated her one-hundredth birthday in 1958 and died the following year at her daughter's home in North Carolina. William Robert, now past seventy-five, has retired from his post as executive director of the Urban League in Warren, Ohio. His grandson, Michael, is a corporal in the Marine Corps and his granddaughter, Linda, teaches in a school in Washington, D.C.

None of Robert Smalls' descendants live in Beaufort. Except for paved roads and a bridge that takes the place of the Lady's Island ferry, the city still looks as it did in General's time. The graceful old homes with the high ceilings and broad piazzas are still there.

So are the live oaks and magnolias, the yellow jessamine in spring and the pink crepe myrtle in fall.

Beaufort still looks the same, but a white couple now owns the house on Prince Street and the homes that freedmen bought at Civil War tax sales are almost all in white hands. The old colored school on Carteret is gone, torn down in the twenties to make way for a white elementary school. The Negro grade school is on the edge of town, next door to the Robert Smalls High School.

Once only a street separated the white and colored children and they met to talk and play together. In the decades after Robert Smalls' death, a wall, high but invisible, divided Beaufort. Negroes were not allowed in the Sea Island Hotel where Smalls had once greeted General Grant. They were not permitted to use the library whose books Robert Smalls had fought to recover. They were ordered to the rear of the buses and to the gallery of the movie theater near the old customs house building on Bay Street. Barred from all but the lowliest jobs, many Beaufort Negroes left home for the cities of the North and West.

The wall is still high, but cracks have begun to appear in it. After Congress passed the Civil Rights Act of 1964, the "White" and "Colored" signs in public places were taken down, and Negroes were able to vote again. In Beaufort today, black citizens are demanding an integrated education for their children. They have boycotted downtown businesses in order to win more and better jobs. Some Negro children —although still less than ten per cent—have been accepted in the "white" schools. Some Negroes have been hired as clerks in stores. For the first time in more than a half-century a Negro sits on Beaufort's

City Council and three black men have been elected to the Beaufort County Council.

Were Robert Smalls to return to Beaufort he would still be a man of hope.

Some Notes and a Bibliography

This is a true story. Because no full-length biography of Robert Smalls was written during his lifetime it has been necessary to piece it together from old newspapers and books, government records, letters, and the recollections of his family and friends. All of the quotations from newspapers, from Army and Navy records, and from speeches are reported accurately. Wherever possible, Robert Smalls' own words have been used. In order to write the story in narrative form, some liberties have been taken in reconstructing conversations and in describing Lydia and Robert Smalls' lives as slaves. Even these reconstructions, however, have been based on extensive research and are accurate in spirit if not in every detail.

The author would like to express particular appreciation to William Robert Smalls, who, in the course of two visits and dozens of letters, related all that he recalled of his father's life and personality. Special thanks should also go to Mrs. Elizabeth Bampfield Hall, daughter of Elizabeth Smalls Bampfield.

Many thanks are due to the residents of Beaufort, South Carolina: to Miss Mabel Runnette, of the Beaufort Township Library, who patiently answered query after query; to Mrs. John Foster, a relative of the McKee family; to Mrs. Beulah Fisher and Mrs. Julius I. Washington, contemporaries of Robert Smalls; to Miss Etta Washington, Miss Lottie Wright, Mrs. Jennie Jackson, and Dr. and Mrs. M. R. Kennedy, who remember General Smalls speaking in their school assemblies; to Mrs. Helen Christensen; and to Captain and Mrs. Paul Cassard, the present owners of the house on Prince Street, who kindly permitted a tour of their home.

Grateful acknowledgement is also given to the librarians of the Rye Free Reading Room; the Schomburg Collection; the New York Public Library; the Library of Congress, Manuscripts Division; to Mrs. Dorothy Porter, librarian of the Moorland Foundation, Howard University; to Miss Sarah Gray, Manuscript Department, Duke University Library; to J. H. Easterby, Director, South Carolina Archives Department; to the Bureau of Customs, Treasury Department; to the National Arhives and Records Service; as well as to Professor George Tindall, author of *South Carolina Negroes 1877–1900,* and Milton Meltzer, co-author of *A Pictorial History of the Negro in America,* for their suggestions about source material.

Special acknowledgement is due to Philip, Peter and Anne Sterling for their critical reading of the manuscript and for their patience and forbearance while the book was in its final stages.

The story of Robert Smalls has been assembled from the following sources:

Biographies of Robert Smalls

COWLEY, CHARLES. *The Romance of History in "The Black County" and The Romance of War in the Career of General Robert Smalls.* Lowell, Mass., 1882.

MILLER, THOMAS. "General Robert Smalls, Hero and Congressman." Speech delivered February 10, 1930, on occasion of doing honor to the Negro member of Congress, Oscar De Priest, and the former Congressmen of African blood. Manuscript.

QUICK, WILLIAM H. *Negro Stars in All Ages*. Richmond, Va., 1898.

SIMKINS, FRANCIS B. in *Dictionary of American Biography*, Vol. 17, New York, 1935.

SIMMONS, WILLIAM. *Men of Mark*. Cleveland, 1887.

SMALLS, WILLIAM ROBERT. "Robert Smalls." Manuscript.

SMITH, ARTHUR J. *The Negro in the Political Classics of the American Government*. Washington, 1937.

United States Naval Training Station. *Great Lakes Bulletin*. Great Lakes, Ill., August 20, 1943.

WOODSON, CARTER. "Robert Smalls and His Descendants," *Negro History Bulletin*, November, 1947.

SLAVERY DAYS

Books:

An Account of the Late Intended Insurrection Among a Portion of the Blacks of this City. Charleston, 1822.

BEAUFORT COUNTY CHAMBER OF COMMERCE. *Beaufort County, South Carolina*. Beaufort, 1953.

BIRNEY, CATHERINE H. *The Grimké Sisters*. Boston, 1885.

CARDOZO, J. N. *Reminiscences of Charleston*. Charleston, 1866.

Charleston City Guide. Charleston, 1872.

Charleston Ordinances. Charleston, 1859.

DU BOIS, W. E. B. *The Suppression of the African Slave-Trade to the United States*. New York, 1954.

FITCHETT, E. HORACE. "Free Negro in South Carolina," *Journal of Negro History*, April, 1940.

"Origin and Growth of Free Negro Population of Charleston," *Journal of Negro History*, October, 1941.

FONER, PHILIP, ED. *The Life and Writings of Frederick Douglass*. Vol. 2. New York, 1951.

Bibliography

FRASER, CHARLES. *Reminiscences of Charleston.* Charleston, 1854.

GRAYSON, WILLIAM J. *James L. Pettigru.* New York, 1866.

JOHNSON, GUION. *A Social History of the Sea Islands.* Chapel Hill, 1930.

JOHNSON, GUY. *Folk Culture on St. Helena Island.* Chapel Hill, 1930.

List of the Taxpayers of the City of Charleston for 1859. Charleston, 1860.

MOLLOY, ROBERT. *Charleston, A Gracious Heritage.* New York, 1947.

OLMSTED, FREDERICK. *A Journey in the Seaboard Slave States.* New York, 1904.

PIERCE, EDWARD. *The Freedmen of Port Royal.* New York, 1863.
"The Freedmen at Port Royal," *The Atlantic Monthly,* September, 1863.

RAVENEL, MRS. ST. JULIEN. *Charleston the Place and the People.* New York, 1931.

SNOWDEN, YATES. *History of South Carolina.* Five vols. New York, 1920.

WALLACE, DAVID DUNCAN. *The History of South Carolina.* Four vols. New York, 1934.

WOOFTER, THOMAS. *Black Yeomanry.* New York, 1930.

WRITERS' PROGRAM OF THE WPA. *South Carolina: A Guide to the Palmetto State.* New York, 1941.

Unpublished Material:

Letters from Miss Mabel Runnette, Beaufort Township Library, to author.

CIVIL WAR

Books:
APTHEKER, HERBERT. *To Be Free.* New York, 1948.

238

Bibliography

BOYNTON, CHARLES. *History of the Navy During the Rebellion*. Two vols. New York, 1867–68.

BROWN, WILLIAM WELLS. *The Black Man*. Boston, 1863.
The Negro in the American Rebellion. Boston, 1867.

CHESNUT, MARY BOYKIN. *A Diary from Dixie*. New York, 1905.

COFFIN, CHARLES CARLETON. *Four Years of Fighting*. Boston, 1866.
Marching to Victory. New York, 1889.

COWLEY, CHARLES. *Leaves from a Lawyer's Life Afloat and Ashore*. Lowell, Mass., 1879.

DAVIS, JEFFERSON. *The Rise and Fall of the Confederate Government*. Two vols. New York, 1881.

DRAPER, JOHN W. *History of the American Civil War*. Vol. 3. New York, 1870.

DU BOIS, W. E. B. *The Gift of Black Folk*. Boston, 1924.

DU PONT, SAMUEL F. *Official Dispatches and Letters*. Wilmington, 1883.

EMILIO, LUIS. *A Brave Black Regiment*. Boston, 1891.

FRAZIER, E. FRANKLIN. *The Negro in the United States*. New York, 1949.

GILLMORE, GENERAL Q. A. "The Army Before Charleston," *Battles and Leaders of the Civil War*. Vol. 4. New York, 1894.

GREELEY, HORACE. *The American Conflict*. Two vols. Chicago, 1866.

HEYWARD, DU BOSE. *Peter Ashley*. New York, 1932.

HIGGINSON, THOMAS W. *Army Life in a Black Regiment*. Boston, 1870.

HUNTER, DAVID. *Report of the Military Services of General David Hunter*. New York, 1873.

JONES, KATHERINE M., ED. *Heroines of Dixie*. New York, 1955.

LESLIE, FRANK. *Illustrated History of the Civil War*. New York, 1895.

LEWIS, LLOYD. *Sherman, Fighting Prophet*. New York, 1932.

MACARTNEY, CLARENCE. *Mr. Lincoln's Admirals.* New York, 1956.

MCPHERSON, EDWARD. *The Political History of the United States of America During the Great Rebellion.* Washington, 1882.

MOORE, FRANK, ED. *The Civil War in Song and Story.* New York, 1889.

    The Rebellion Record. 12 vols. New York, 1861–68.

MYERS, WILLIAM STARR. *The Republican Party.* New York, 1928.

NICHOLS, GEORGE W. *The Story of the Great March.* New York, 1866.

PARIS, COMTE DE. *History of the Civil War in America.* Vol. 2. Philadelphia, 1876.

PORTER, DAVID D. *The Naval History of the Civil War.* New York, 1886.

PRATT, FLETCHER. *A Short History of the Civil War.* New York, 1952.

QUARLES, BENJAMIN. *The Negro in the Civil War.* Boston, 1953.

RANDALL, JAMES G. *Civil War and Reconstruction.* Boston, 1937.

ROSS, ISHBEL. *Angel of the Battlefield.* New York, 1956.

RUSSELL, WILLIAM H. *My Diary North and South.* New York, 1954.

TAYLOR, SUSIE KING. *Reminiscences of My Life in Camp.* Boston, 1902.

United States. *Congressional Globe.* Thirty-seventh Congress, second session.

    Congressional Record. Fifty-fifth Congress, second session, Report No. 120.

    Official Records of the Union and Confederate Navies in the War of the Rebellion. Series I, Vols. 12, 13, 28, 35. Washington, 1894–1922.

    The War of the Rebellion: Official Records of Union and Confederate Armies. Series I, Vols. 6, 14, 16, 47; Series III, Vol. 2. Washington, 1880–1901.

WELLES, GIDEON. *Diary of Gideon Welles.* Boston, 1911.

WESLEY, CHARLES. *Collapse of the Confederacy.* Washington, 1937.

WILEY, BELL. *Southern Negroes, 1861–65.* New Haven, 1938.

WILLIAMS, GEORGE WASHINGTON. *History of the Negro Troops in the War of the Rebellion.* New York, 1888.

WILSON, JOSEPH T. *The Black Phalanx.* Hartford, 1888.

Newspapers and Magazines:

Beaufort *Free South,* 1863–64.

Charleston *Daily Courier,* May 14, 1862.

Columbia *Daily Union Herald,* January, 1875.

The Commonwealth, September, 1862–January, 1864.

The Crisis, April, 1949. "The 'Abduction' of the Planter," by James M. Rosbow.

Douglass' Monthly. May–September, 1862.

Harper's Weekly, May–June, 1862; April–October, 1863.

The Liberator, May, 1862–December, 1865.

National Anti-Slavery Standard, May, 1862–May, 1865.

New York *Daily Tribune,* May–August, 1862; November–December, 1863; May–June, 1864.

New York *Evening Post,* May–August, 1862; February–April, 1864.

The Palmetto Herald, March–November, 1864.

Port Royal *New South,* August, 1862–April, 1864.

Washington *National Republican,* May–June, 1862.

Weekly Anglo-African, November, 1860–August, 1861.

Unpublished Material:

United States National Archives and Records Service. Records of Smalls and the *Planter,* 1862–66.

    Navy Department. Letters to Robert Smalls Bampfield and author.

    War Department. Letters to Robert Smalls Bampfield and author.

FREEDMEN

BOTUME, ELIZABETH. *First Days Among the Contrabands.* Boston, 1893.

First Annual Report of the Educational Commission for Freedmen. Boston, 1863.

FORTEN, CHARLOTTE. *The Journal of Charlotte Forten.* Edited by Ray A. Billington. New York, 1953.

FRENCH, MRS. A. M. *Slavery in South Carolina and Ex-Slaves.* New York, 1862.

FRENCH, MANSFIELD. *Address to Masters and Freedmen.* Macon, 1865.

MCKIM, J. MILLER. *The Freedmen of South Carolina.* Philadelphia, 1862.

NORDHOFF, CHARLES. *The Freedmen of South Carolina.* New York, 1863.

PEARSON, ELIZABETH, ED. *Letters from Port Royal, 1862–68.* Boston, 1906.

WASHINGTON AND NEW YORK, 1862

Books:

BROOKS, NOAH. *Abraham Lincoln and the Downfall of American Slavery.* New York, 1896.

CARPENTER, FRANCIS. *Inner Life of Abraham Lincoln.* New York, 1868.

FEDERAL WRITERS' PROJECT, WPA. *Washington City and Capital.* Washington, 1937.

New York City Guide. New York, 1939.

FLOWER, FRANK. *Edwin McMasters Stanton.* Akron, 1905.

FRENCH, MANSFIELD JOSEPH. *Ancestors and Descendants of Samuel French.* Ann Arbor, 1940.

HERTZ, EMANUEL. *Lincoln Talks.* New York, 1939.

KECKLEY, ELIZABETH. *Behind the Scenes.* New York, 1868.

LEECH, MARGARET. *Reveille in Washington, 1861–65.* New York, 1941.

LELAND, CHARLES. *Abraham Lincoln.* New York, 1885.

NICOLAY, HELEN. *Personal Traits of Abraham Lincoln.* New York, 1912.

NICOLAY AND HAY. *Abraham Lincoln: A History.* Vols. 4–9. New York, 1890.

RAYMOND, HENRY. *The Life and Public Services of Abraham Lincoln.* New York, 1865.

SANDBURG, CARL. *Abraham Lincoln: The War Years.* Four vols. New York, 1939.

THOMAS, BENJAMIN P. *Abraham Lincoln.* New York, 1952.

United States. *Congressional Record.* Forty-ninth Congress, first session. Appendix, p. 320.

WARDEN, ROBERT B. *An Account of the Private Life and Public Services of Salmon P. Chase.* Cincinnati, 1874.

WILSON, HENRY. *The History of the Rise and Fall of the Slave Power in America.* Vol. 3. Boston, 1872–77.

Newspapers and Magazines:

New York *Daily Tribune,* September–October, 1862.

New York *Evening Post,* September–October, 1862.

Washington *Daily National Intelligencer,* August, 1862.

Washington *National Republican,* August, 1862.

PHILADELPHIA, 1864

Books:

DU BOIS, W. E. B. *The Philadelphia Negro.* Philadelphia, 1899.

KAUFFMAN, JAMES. *Philadelphia's Navy Yards.* New York, 1948.

Reports of the Committee Appointed for the Purpose of Securing to the Colored People in Philadelphia the Right to the Use of the Street Cars. Philadelphia, 1867.

Republican Party. *Proceedings of the National Union Convention held in Baltimore,* June 7–8, 1864.

SPIERS, FREDERICK. *Street Railway System of Philadelphia.* Baltimore, 1898.

STILL, WILLIAM. *A Brief Narrative of the Struggle for the Rights of the Colored People of Philadelphia in the City Railway Cars.* Philadelphia, 1867.

TAYLOR, FRANK H. *Philadelphia in the Civil War.* Philadelphia, 1913.

Newspapers and Magazines:

The A. M. E. Church Review, January–March, 1955. "Captain Robert Smalls Addresses the General Conference of 1864."

Philadelphia *Press,* May, 1864–January, 1865.

New Orleans *Tribune,* February 16, 1865.

Unpublished Material:

National Archives, Washington. Records of the *Planter,* 1864.

FALL OF CHARLESTON

Books:

COFFIN, CHARLES CARLETON. *Freedom Triumphant.* New York, 1891.

FRENCH, J. C., AND CARY, EDWARD. *Trip of the Steamer Oceanus to Fort Sumter and Charleston, S. C.* New York, 1865.

GARRISON, W. P., AND F. J. *William Lloyd Garrison. The Story of His Life as Told by His Children.* Vol. 4. Boston and New York, 1894.

REID, WHITELAW. *After the War: A Southern Tour.* London, 1886.

ROLLIN, FRANK. *Life and Public Services of Martin R. Delany.* Boston, 1883.

WILLIAMS, G. W. *St. Michael's, Charleston.* Columbia, 1951.

Bibliography

Newspapers and Magazines:
Charleston *Daily Courier*, April 15–17, 1865.
Harper's Weekly, March–April, 1865.
New York *Daily Tribune*, February–April, 1865.

RECONSTRUCTION

Books:
ALLEN, WALTER. *Governor Chamberlain's Administration in South Carolina.* New York, 1888.

ALVORD, J. W. *Letters from the South Relating to the Condition of Freedmen.* Washington, 1870.

BANCROFT, FREDERIC. *A Sketch of the Negro in Politics, especially in South Carolina and Mississippi.* New York, 1885.

BLAINE, JAMES G. *Twenty Years of Congress.* Vol. 2. Norwich, Conn., 1884.

COOLEY, ROSSA B. *Homes of the Freed.* New York, 1926.
School Acres. New Haven, 1930.

DAVIS, VARINA. *Jefferson Davis.* New York, 1890.

DE FOREST, JOHN. *A Union Officer in the Reconstruction.* New Haven, 1948.

DU BOIS, W. E. B. *Black Reconstruction.* New York, 1935.

FONER, PHILIP, ED. *The Life and Writings of Frederick Douglass.* Vol. 4. New York, 1955.

GREEN, JOHN P. *Recollections of the Inhabitants, Localities, Superstitions and Ku Klux Outrages of the Carolinas.* Cleveland, 1880.

HOLLIS, JOHN P. *The Early Period of Reconstruction in South Carolina.* Baltimore, 1905.

HOWARD, OLIVER O. *Autobiography of O. O. Howard.* New York, 1907.

HUGHES, LANGSTON, AND MELTZER, MILTON. *A Pictorial History of the Negro in America.* New York, 1956.

JARRELL, HAMPTON M. *Wade Hampton and the Negro.* Columbia, 1949.

KING, EDWARD. *The Southern States of North America.* Hartford, 1875.

LYNCH, JOHN. *The Facts of Reconstruction.* New York, 1913. *Some Historical Errors of James Ford Rhodes.* Boston, 1922.

PIERCE, PAUL. *The Freedmen's Bureau.* Iowa City, 1904.

QUARLES, BENJAMIN. *Frederick Douglass.* Washington, 1948.

Republican Party. *Proceedings of the National Union Republican Convention Held in Chicago, May 20–21, 1868. National Convention, June 14–16, 1876.*

Republican Party of South Carolina. *Reply to the Memorial of the Taxpayers Convention.* Columbia, 1874.

REYNOLDS, JOHN. *Reconstruction in South Carolina.* Columbia, 1905.

ROWLAND, ERON. *Varina Howell, Wife of Jefferson Davis.* Vol. 2. New York, 1931.

SCHAFF, MORRIS. *Jefferson Davis, His Life and Personality.* Boston, 1922.

SCHURTZ, CARL. *Reminiscences.* Vol. 3. New York, 1907.

SIMKINS, FRANCIS, AND WOODY, ROBERT. *South Carolina During Reconstruction.* Chapel Hill, 1932.

South Carolina. *Proceedings of the Constitutional Convention of South Carolina, held at Charleston, January 14–March 17, 1868.* Charleston, 1868. *Journal of the House of Representatives, 1873–74.* Columbia, 1874. *Journal of the Senate, 1870–75.* Columbia, 1871–75.

STEARNS, CHARLES. *The Black Man of the South.* New York, 1872.

SWANBERG, W. A. *Sickles the Incredible.* New York, 1956.

SWINT, HENRY L. *The Northern Teacher in the South.* Nashville, 1941.

TAYLOR, ALRUTHEUS. *The Negro in South Carolina During Reconstruction.* Washington, 1924.

TOWNE, LAURA. *Letters and Diary of Laura M. Towne.* Edited by R. S. Holland. Boston, 1912.

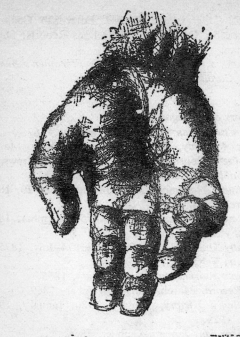

TROWBRIDGE, J. T. *A Picture of the Desolated States.* Hartford, 1868.

United States. *Congressional Record.* Forty-fifth Congress, second session. Committee of Elections Reports: Smalls vs. Tillman.

WEBSTER, LAURA J. *The Operation of the Freedmen's Bureau in South Carolina.* Northampton, 1916.

Newspapers and Magazines:

The American Freedman, April, 1866–January, 1867.

The Atlantic Monthly, February, 1866. "Three Months Among the Reconstructionists," by Sidney Andrews.

Beaufort *Republican,* October, 1871–October, 1873.

Beaufort *Tribune,* November 25, 1874–December 20, 1876.

Charleston *Free Press,* April 4, 1868.

Charleston *News and Courier,* May, 1875–December, 1876.

Columbia *Daily Register,* April 6, 1884.

Columbia *Daily Union Herald,* October, 1874–July, 1875.

Columbia *State,* February 25, 1901.

The Freedmen's Journal, January–February, 1865.

Freedmen's Record, March, 1865–November, 1869.

Journal of Negro History, January, 1920; January, 1923; January, 1925.

The Loyal Georgian, January–October, 1866.

National Anti-Slavery Standard, June, 1865–May, 1867.

The National Freedman, December, 1865–July, 1866.

New York *Daily Tribune,* October, 1876.

Port Royal *Commercial,* October, 1873–April, 1874.

Savannah *Tribune,* December, 1875–December, 1876.

South Atlantic Quarterly, October, 1919. "Reconstruction and Education in South Carolina," by Edgar W. Knight.

Weekly Anglo-African, August–December, 1865.

Unpublished Material:

South Carolina Archives Department. Letters from Robert Smalls.

CONGRESS

Books:

BLAINE, JAMES. *Twenty of Years of Congress.* Norwich, Conn., 1884.

COX, SAMUEL. *Three Decades of Federal Legislation.* Providence, 1886.

GOSNELL, HAROLD. *Negro Politicians.* Chicago, 1935.

LANGSTON, JOHN MERCER. *From the Virginia Plantation to the National Capitol.* Hartford, 1894.

MCCLURE, ALEXANDER K. *Recollections of Half a Century.* Salem, 1902.

SHERMAN, JOHN. *Recollections of Forty Years in the House, Senate and Cabinet.* Two vols. Chicago, 1895.

SMITH, SAMUEL DENNY. *The Negro in Congress.* Chapel Hill, 1940.

United States. *Biographical Directory of the American Congress. Congressional Record,* 44th, 45th, 47th, 48th, 49th, 50th, 56th Congresses.
    House Reports, 50th Congress. Robert Smalls vs. William Elliott.
    Ku Klux Conspiracy. Washington, 1872.

Newspapers and Magazines:

The Bee, 1882–89.

Charleston *News and Courier,* October 16–November 4, 1886.

Ebony, May, 1956. "Negro Senators from Mississippi."

The Grit, December, 1883–October, 1884.

Journal of Negro History, April, 1922. "Negro Congressmen a Generation After," by A. A. Taylor.

1877–96

Books:

BRUCE, J. E. *Reply to Senator Wade Hampton's Article in The Forum for June.* N.p., n.d.

Bibliography

CABLE, GEORGE WASHINGTON. *The Silent South*. New York, 1907.

CAMPBELL, SIR GEORGE. *White and Black*. London, 1879.

FORTUNE, T. THOMAS. *Black and White: Land, Labor and Politics in the South*. New York, 1884.

FRANKLIN, JOHN HOPE. *From Slavery to Freedom*. New York, 1947.

KEY, V. O., JR. *Southern Politics in State and Nation*. New York, 1949.

LEWINSON, PAUL. *Race, Class and Party: A History of Negro Suffrage and White Politics in the South*. New York, 1932.

LOGAN, R. W. *Negro in American Life and Thought, The Nadir, 1877–1901*. New York, 1954.

MANGUM, CHARLES. *The Legal Status of the Negro*. Chapel Hill, 1940.

MILLER, MARY, ED. *Suffrage Speeches by Negroes in the Constitutional Convention*. N.p., n.d.

NEWS AND COURIER, ED. *South Carolina in 1884*. Charleston, 1884.

RAPER, ARTHUR F. *The Tragedy of Lynching*. Chapel Hill, 1933.

Republican Party. *Convention Proceedings, 1880–96*.
Republican Campaign Textbooks, 1878–1908.

SIMKINS, FRANCIS. *Pitchfork Ben Tillman*. Baton Rouge, 1944.
Tillman Movement in South Carolina. Durham, 1926.

SMALLS, SARAH. *Speeches at the Constitutional Convention by General Robert Smalls*. Charleston, 1896.

South Carolina. *Journal of the Constitutional Convention*. Columbia, 1895.
Report of the Attorney General to the General Assembly for the fiscal year ending October 31, 1877. Columbia, 1878.
Report of the Joint Investigating Committee on Public Frauds. Columbia, 1878.

TINDALL, GEORGE B. *South Carolina Negroes 1877–1900*. Columbia, 1952.

Bibliography

United States House of Representatives. *Testimony on Recent Elections in South Carolina.* Washington, 1877.

WOODSON, CARTER. *The Negro in Our History.* Washington, 1931.

WOODWARD, C. VANN. *Origins of the New South, 1877–1913.* Baton Rouge, 1951.
Reunion and Reaction. Boston, 1951.

Newspapers and Magazines:

Annals of the American Academy of Political and Social Science, September, 1913. "Fifty Years of Freedom: Conditions in the Sea Coast Regions," by Neils Christensen.

The Atlantic Monthly, February–June, 1877.

Boston *Daily Advertiser,* May 13–16, 1882.

Boston *Herald,* May 16, 1882.

Charleston *News and Courier,* October, 1877–June, 1896.

Journal of Negro History, October, 1922; July, 1952.

Journal of Southern History, February, May, 1936; May, 1949.

New York *Daily Tribune,* 1877–89.

New York *World,* July, 1889; September–October, 1895.

North American Review, November, 1890. "Election Methods in the South," by Robert Smalls.

Port Royal *Palmetto Post,* 1882–96.

Washington *National Republican,* July 22, 1878.

Unpublished Material:

Duke University. George Gage Papers.

South Carolina Archives Department. Letters from Robert Smalls.

1896–1915

Books:

ADAMS, CYRUS F. *The Republican Party and the Afro-American.* New York, 1912.

Bibliography

BEAUFORT, S. C. *First Annual Report of the City Council.* Beaufort, 1916.

MILLER, KELLY. *Roosevelt and the Negro.* Washington, 1907.

MYERS, WILLIAM STARR. *The Republican Party.* New York, 1928.

Republican Party. *Proceedings of 1896 Convention in St. Louis.*

SCHMECKEBIER, LAURENCE F. *The Customs Service.* Baltimore, 1924.

United States. *Congressional Record,* 54th and 56th Congresses.

National Cemeteries. Washington, 1874.

WOODWARD, C. VANN. *The Strange Career of Jim Crow.* New York, 1955.

Newspapers and Magazines:

Charleston *News and Courier,* June 14, 1896.

The Crisis, April, 1915.

Journal of Negro History, October, 1920.

New York *Age,* March 4, 1915.

Savannah *Tribune,* March 6, 1915.

Southern Workman, October, 1903. "The Negroes of Beaufort County, South Carolina," by Neils Christensen.

Unpublished Material:

Howard University. Moorland Foundation. Miscellaneous newspaper clippings.

United States. Library of Congress. Carter Woodson Collection.

tion. Letters from Robert Smalls.

Treasury Department, Bureau of Customs. Letters to the author.

Index

Index

About the Author and Illustrator

Dorothy Sterling has written many successful and highly praised nonfiction books for young people, including *Freedom Train*, a biography of Harriet Tubman. Not only is she a good writer, but she is also a thorough researcher. To gather the facts and background information for *Captain of the Planter*, she visited Charleston and Beaufort, where she read old newspapers and talked to old-timers who had known Mr. Smalls; had two visits from William Robert Smalls, who talked of his father and gave her old clippings and photographs; delved into newspaper files, library collections, and archives.

Ernest Crichlow, painter and illustrator, also talked to William Robert Smalls, and he used the material which Mrs. Sterling had gathered during her research—including many old prints and photos—to make his pictures accurate.